THE **POCKET IDIOT'S GUIDE**™ TO

Spanish Phrases

Second Edition

by Gail Stein

ALPHA

A member of Penguin Group (USA) Inc.

This book is dedicated to my patient, proofreader husband, Douglas; my skilled, computer-consultant son, Eric; my most ardent fan and son, Michael; and my parents, Sara and Jack Bernstein, whose love and support have helped me become the woman I am today.

Copyright © 2003 by Gail Stein

THE POCKET IDIOT'S GUIDE TO and Design are registered trademarks of Penguin Group (USA) Inc.

International Standard Book Number: 0-02-864444-1
Library of Congress Catalog Card Number: 2002115714

05 04 03   8 7 6 5 4 3

Interpretation of the printing code: The rightmost number of the first series of numbers is the year of the book's printing; the rightmost number of the second series of numbers is the number of the book's printing. For example, a printing code of 02-1 shows that the first printing occurred in 2002.

Printed in the United States of America

Contents

Introduction

Your travel plans include a visit to a Spanish-speaking country or two. Or business opportunities beckon and abound in a Spanish-speaking land. Or your love of languages is driving you to continue your studies. Whether you're traveling, working, or just a student at heart, you want to brush up on your Spanish and you want to do it *now*. Or perhaps you've never studied the language and you need an intensive crash course.

Take a long, hard look around you—Spanish is everywhere. There's no time like the present to familiarize yourself with words, phrases, and expressions that can come in handy on a daily basis. In no time flat, you'll appreciate the advantages that a knowledge of Spanish can bring you, no matter what the situation.

What's on the Inside

So you want to speak Spanish. Is it because a sexy, Latino accent makes your heart skip a beat and your legs start to wobble? Perhaps it's because the aroma of fine, home-cooked paella makes your stomach growl in eager anticipation of an extraordinary repast. Or is it because seductive ads containing the beautiful white sands and blue waters of Cancun's beaches beckon you at vacation time? Whatever your reasons for wanting to learn the language, this book will help you achieve quick and easy results.

You will learn pronunciation and grammar painlessly and effortlessly without sacrificing speed and accuracy. Whether you're a student, a traveler, or a business person, this book will teach you the basics while giving you the vocabulary and the phrases you'll find most useful in almost every conceivable daily situation. You'll be introduced to a wide variety of topics: food, clothing, sports, health, and much more.

This book is not merely a phrase book, a grammar text, or a travel guide—it's a combination of all three. That makes it not only very unique but an extremely useful tool for people who want a working command of the Spanish language. It will allow you to understand and to be understood without embarrassment or frustration and with ease and enjoyment. Yes, learning Spanish can be fun!

This book was written with you in mind. That's why it's so user-friendly. By the time you've read it through, you'll be a pro at ordering a meal to suit your diet, watching a Spanish film without depending on the subtitles, finding the perfect meringue partner, and replacing the contact lens you lost while scuba diving. You'll be amazed and surprised at how rapidly you'll learn what you need to know.

In addition to all the vocabulary lists, phrases, grammatical explanations, references, and pronunciation guides, this book contains lots of extras presented in sidebars throughout the text:

Something Extra _____

Look here for extra tips and hints about the language.

¡Cuidado! _____

Watch out! These boxes indicate pitfalls and traps you want to sidestep.

Acknowledgments

Thank you! Thank you! Thank you to some very special people who have made a difference in my life and have greatly enriched it. A special "I love you!" accompanied by hugs and kisses to:

Ray Elias for ensuring that the local bookstores keep Stein in stock and for being an even greater guy 38 years later.

Roger H. Herz for being a fabulous consultant.

Marty Hyman for giving me the best legal advice imaginable.

Chris Levy for being the best advisor and confidante in the world.

And thanks to the people at Alpha Books.

Trademarks

All terms mentioned in this book that are known to be or are suspected of being trademarks or service marks have been appropriately capitalized. Alpha Books and Penguin Group (USA) Inc. cannot attest to the accuracy of this information. Use of a term in this book should not be regarded as affecting the validity of any trademark or service mark.

The Gringo's Quick Pronunciation Guide

Even though Spanish is a foreign language, it's very easy to pronounce because it is very phonetic. It's that simple! Just say each word exactly as you see it and add a Spanish accent. Chances are, you'll sound remarkably like a native speaker—well, close to one anyway.

Accentuate the Positive

You will notice that there are three accents in Spanish:

- The ´ simply indicates that you put more stress on the vowel.

- The ~ only appears over an n. It produces the sound "ny" as in the first "n" in "union." The ñ in considered a separate letter.

- The ¨ can be used when there is a diphthong (two vowels together). It indicates that each vowel must be pronounced separately.

¡Cuidado!

All letters in Spanish are pronounced except the letter *h*, which is always silent. The letter *v* is pronounced like the English *b*. The *k* and the *w* are used only in words of foreign origin.

Different Strokes for Different Folks

The following pronunciations are for the Spanish spoken in South and Central America and in certain areas of southern Spain.

Letter	Sound	Example	Pronunciation
Vowels			
a	ah	Ana	ah-nah
e	eh	entrar	ehn-trahr
i	ee	idea	ee-deh-yah
o	oh	oficina	oh-fee-see-nah
u	oo	usar	oo-sahr
Diphthongs (Vowel Combinations)			
ae	ah-yeh	aeropuerto	ah-yeh-roh-pwehr-toh
ai	ah-yee	aire	ah-yee-reh
au	ow	auto	ow-toh
ay	ahy	hay	ahy
ea	eh-yah	reacción	rreh-yahk-see-yohn
ei	eh-yee	beisból	beh-yees-bohl
eo	eh-yoh	feo	feh-yoh
eu	eh-yoo	Europa	eh-yoo-roh-pah
ey	eh-yee	rey	rreh-yee
ia	ee-yah	Gloria	gloh-ree-yah
ie	ee-yeh	fiesta	fee-yehs-tah
io	ee-yoh	avión	ah-bee-yohn
iu	ee-yoo	ciudad	see-yoo-dahd
oa	oh-wah	toalla	toh-wah-yah
oe	oh-weh	oeste	oh-wehs-teh

Letter	Sound	Example	Pronunciation
oi	oy	oiga	oy-gah
oy	oy	soy	soy
ua	wah	guardar	gwahr-dahr
ue	weh	cuesta	kwehs-tah
ui	wee	cuidado	kwee-dah-doh
uo	oo-oh	conintuo	kohn-tee-noo-oh
uy	wee	muy	mwee

Consonants

b	b	bueno	bweh-noh
c	soft c (s) before e, i	centro	sehn-troh
	hard c (k) elsewhere	casa	kah-sah
ch	ch	Chile	chee-leh
d	d	dos	dohs
f	f	favor	fah-bohr
g	soft g before e, i	general	heh-neh-rahl
	hard g elsewhere	gracias	grah-see-yahs
h	silent	hombre	ohm-breh
k	k	kilo	kee-loh
l	l	lista	lees-tah
ll	y	llama	yah-mah
m	m	madre	mah-dreh
n	n	nada	nah-dah
ñ	ny	año	ah-nyoh
p	p	padre	pah-dreh

continues

Letter	Sound	Example	Pronunciation
q	k	Quito	kee-toh
r	r (small roll)	salero	sah-leh-roh
rr	r (large roll)	carro	kah-rroh
s	s	sí	see
t	t	toro	toh-roh
v	b (less explosive English b)	vender	behn-dehr
x	s, ks	extra	ehs-trah
		exacto	ehk-sahk-toh
z	s	zoo	so

Something Extra

The Spanish r is always rolled. Give it something extra when the r comes at the beginning of the word. The rr is always rolled a lot (about three trills).

Chapter 1

A Plan of Action

In This Chapter

- Getting off to a good start
- What you already know
- Idiomatic Spanish

So you want to learn Spanish and you want to learn it fast. The easiest and most efficient way to accomplish this goal is just to plunge right in. Totally immerse yourself in anything and everything Spanish. The trick is to have a love affair not only with the language but with the culture as well. Follow these suggestions if you want to quickly develop a long-lasting, fulfilling relationship with Spanish.

- Be honest with yourself. What exactly are your goals? How much linguistic ability do you possess? Do you have a good ear for language? Determine how much time each day you want to devote to Spanish and stick with it. Proceed at your own pace. There's no rush!

- One way or another, get your hands on a good bilingual dictionary. Pocket varieties (which usually cost between $6 and $15) might suit the needs of some learners but can prove somewhat deficient for others. The following are among the more popular, easy-to-use, and comprehensive dictionaries, with a wide range of up-to-the-minute, colloquial, and idiomatic words and phrases:

  HarperCollins (approximately $55)

  Larousse (approximately $60)

- Listen to Spanish whenever you can. Never miss an opportunity to become involved with the language. A wide selection of foreign films is available at large video stores. Public service radio and television broadcast many Spanish programs. Look and listen! Borrow language tapes from your local library and pay attention to the sounds of Spanish.

- Read everything you can get your hands on. Read to yourself or out loud to your mirror. Practice your comprehension and your pronunciation all at once. Pick up a Spanish newspaper (*El Diario* or *La Prensa*, for example) and focus on what's happening in the Hispanic world.

- Find the perfect spot in your home to serve as *un rincón español* (a Spanish corner). Dedicate this area to your new project. Make it look the part.

Let Us Begin

Your knowledge of Spanish is undoubtedly more extensive than you realize. That's right. You know more than you think. Chocolate, potatoes, tomatoes, taxi, patio, piano, alpaca, mosquito—the list of Spanish words used in English is surprisingly long!

The Cognate Connection

Want to pick up Spanish really quickly? Learn your cognates! What are they? Quite simply, a *cognate* is a word spelled exactly the same (or almost the same) as a word in English and that has the same meaning. Sometimes we've actually borrowed a word from Spanish, letter for letter, and have incorporated it into our own vocabulary. Sure, cognates are pronounced differently in each language, but the meaning of the Spanish word is quite obvious to anyone who speaks English.

Want to get a jump start on your list? Tables 1.1 and 1.2 provide lists of words that are the same (or almost the same) in both languages.

Table 1.1   Exact Cognates

Adjectives	Masculine Nouns El (ehl)	Feminine Nouns La (lah)
cruel (kroo-ehl)	actor (ahk-tohr)	banana (bah-nah-nah)
grave (grah-beh)	animal (ah-nee-mahl)	fiesta (fee-yehs-tah)

continues

Table 1.1 (continued)

Adjectives	Masculine Nouns El (ehl)	Feminine Nouns La (lah)
horrible (oh-rree-bleh)	color (koh-lohr)	hotel (oh-tehl)
natural (nah-too-rahl)	hospital (ohs-pee-tahl)	radio (rah-dee-yoh)
tropical (troh-pee-kahl)	motor (moh-tohr)	soda (soh-dah)

Table 1.2   Almost Exact Cognates

Adjectives	Masculine Nouns El (ehl)	Feminine Nouns La (lah)
ambicioso (ahm-bee-see-yoh-soh)	aniversario (ah-nee-behr-sah-ree-yoh)	aspirina (ahs-pee-ree-nah)
confortable (kohn-fohr-tah-bleh)	automovíl (ow-toh-moh-beel)	bicicleta (bee-see-kleh-tah)
curioso (koo-ree-yoh-soh)	barbero (bahr-beh-roh)	blusa (bloo-sah)
delicioso (deh-lee-see-yoh-soh)	diccionario (deeks-yoh-nah-ree-yoh)	cathedral (kah-teh-drahl)
diferente (dee-feh rehn-teh)	elefante (eh-leh-fahn-teh)	dieta (dee-yeh-tah)
elegante (eh-leh-gahn-teh)	grupo (groo-poh)	familia (fah-meel-yah)

Adjectives	Masculine Nouns El (ehl)	Feminine Nouns La (lah)
excelente (ehk-seh-lehn-teh)	menú (meh-noo)	gasolina (gah-soh-lee-nah)
importante (eem-pohr-tahn-teh)	parque (pahr-keh)	guitarra (gee-tah-rrah)
imposible (eem-poh-see-bleh)	plato (plah-toh)	hamburguesa (ahm-boor-geh-sah)
moderno (moh-dehr-noh)	presidente (preh-see-dehn-teh)	lista (lees-tah)
necesario (neh-seh-sah-ree-yoh)	profesor (proh-feh-sohr)	música (moo-see-kah)
ordinario (ohr-dee-nah-ree-yoh)	programa (proh-grah-mah)	nacionalidad (nah-see-yoh-nah-lee-dahd)
posible (poh-see-bleh)	restaurante (rrehs-tow-rahn-teh)	opinión (oh-pee-nee-yohn)
probable (proh-bah-bleh)	salario (sah-lah-ree-yoh)	persona (pehr-soh-nah)
rico (rree-koh)	teléfono (teh-leh-foh-noh)	turista (too-rees-tah)
sincero (seen-seh-roh)	tigre (tee-greh)	universidad (oo-nee-behr-see-dahd)

Verbs

Verbs (action words) can be cognates, too. The majority of Spanish verbs fall into one of three categories: the -*ar* family, the -*er* family, and the -*ir* family. These verbs are considered regular because all verbs in the same family follow the same rules.

You should recognize the following verbs. Don't forget to add them to your growing list of cognates.

-AR verbs	-ER verbs	-IR verbs
acompañar (ah-kohm-pah-nyahr)	comprender (kohm-prehn-dehr)	aplaudir (ah-plow-deer)
celebrar (seh-leh-brahr)	responder (rrehs-pohn-dehr)	decidir (deh-see-deer)
declarar (deh-klah-rahr)	vender (behn-dehr)	describir (dehs-kree-beer)
entrar (ehn-trahr)		persuadir (pehr-swah-deer)
observar (ohb-sehr-bahr)		omitir (oh-mee-teer)
preparar (preh-pah-rahr)		recibir (rreh-see-beer)
usar (oo-sahr)		sufrir (soo-freer)

Chapter 2

Grammar 1-2-3

In This Chapter

- Nouns
- Verbs
- Adjectives
- Adverbs
- Prepositions

If you really want to speak Spanish like a native, you will be happy to know that speaking a foreign language doesn't mean you'll have to mentally translate pages of rules. With today's communicative approach, it's simply not necessary for you to walk around with a dictionary under your arm. On the contrary, it means learning to use the language and its patterns naturally, the way a native speaker does. To do this, you need to know basic grammar as well as the idioms and colloquialisms used by native speakers.

Nouns for Names

Nouns name people, places, things, or ideas. Just like in English, nouns can be replaced by pronouns (such as he, she, it, they). Unlike in English, however, all nouns in Spanish have a gender. This means all nouns have a sex. Sex refers to the masculine or feminine designation of the noun. In Spanish, all nouns also have a number (singular or plural). Little articles (words that stand for "the" or "a") serve as noun identifiers and usually help indicate gender and number. Remember, even if you can't figure out the gender of a noun or if you use the wrong gender or number, you will still be understood as long as you use the correct word.

Gender

Gender is very easy in Spanish. All nouns that refer to males are masculine; those that refer to females are feminine. Use the noun identifiers in Table 2.1 to express "the" or "a":

Table 2.1   Singular Noun Identifiers

	the	a, an, one
Masculine	el	un
Feminine	la	una

Some noun endings make it extremely easy to determine the gender. In general, masculine nouns end in -o and feminine nouns end in -a. Table 2.2 provides a list of endings that can help make the job of gender identification easy.

Table 2.2   Gender Identification Made Easy

Masculine	Endings	Feminine	Endings
-o	carro	-a	fiesta
-ema	problema	-ión	porción
-consonants	limón	-dad	oportunidad
(usually)		-tad	amistad
		-tud	juventud
		-umbre	costumbre
		-ie	serie

Something Extra

Some nouns can be either masculine or feminine depending on whether the speaker is referring to a male or female. Just change the article without changing the spelling of the noun:

el artista	*la artista*
el estudiante	*la estudiante*

Some nouns are always just masculine or just feminine no matter the sex of the person to whom you are referring:

el bebé	*la persona*

Of course, there are always exceptions to the rule—just make sure you don't get lazy, sloppy, and over-confident. Keep the following exceptions in mind for future use:

- Masculine nouns that end in -a:

  el clima (ehl klee-mah), the climate

  el día (ehl dee-yah), the day

  el idioma (ehl ee-dee-yoh-mah), the language

  el mapa (ehl mah-pah), the map

  el problema (ehl proh-bleh-mah), the problem

  el programa (ehl proh-grah-mah), the program

  el telegrama (ehl teh-leh-grah-mah), the telegram

- Feminine nouns that end in -o

  la mano (lah mah-noh), the hand

  la radio (lah rrah-dee-yoh), the radio

  la foto, short for *fotografía* (lah foh-toh), the photo

  la moto, short for *motocicleta* (lah moh-toh), the motorcycle

Number

When a Spanish noun refers to more than one person, place, thing, or idea, it must be made plural—just like in English. Table 2.3 shows that it is not enough to simply change the noun. The identifying article must be made plural as well.

Table 2.3   Plural Articles

	the	some
Masculine	los	unos
Feminine	las	unas

Forming the plural of nouns in Spanish is really quite easy. All you have to do is add -*s* to a singular noun that ends in a vowel, and add -*es* to a singular noun that ends in a consonant.

el muchacho	*los muchachos*	*el autor*	*los autores*
la muchacha	*las muchachas*	*la ciudad*	*las ciudades*

Something Extra

No ending is added for nouns already ending in -*s*, except for nouns ending in -*és*:

el jueves   *los jueves*

BUT

el inglés   *los ingleses* (the accent is dropped to maintain original stress)

¡Cuidado!

For nouns ending in -*z*, change the *z* to *c* before adding -*es*:

el pez   *los peces*

una actriz   *unas actrices*

Verbs in Action

Verbs are words that indicate actions or states of being. Verbs require a subject, whether it is expressed in a statement or implied in a command. Subjects can be nouns or pronouns and, just like in English, they are given a person and a number as shown in Table 2.4.

Table 2.4 Subject Pronouns

Person	Singular	Plural
first	yo (yoh), I	nosotros (noh-soh-trohs), we
second	tú (too), you	vosotros (boh-soh-trohs), you
third	él (ehl), he	ellos (eh-yohs), they
	ella (eh-yah), she	ellas (eh-yahs), they
	usted (Ud.) (oo-stehd), you	ustedes (Uds.) (oo-steh-dehs), you

Subject pronouns are not used as often in Spanish as they are in English. This is because the verb ending usually quite clearly identifies the subject.

To speak about a group of women, use *nosotras* or *vosotras* or *ellas*. When speaking about a mixed group, always use the masculine plural—regardless of the number of males in the group.

Tú is used when speaking to a relative, a close friend, a child, or a pet. In all other instances, use the polite form *Ud.* The *vosotros* form is used primarily in Spain. In Spanish-speaking South America and the Caribbean, the *Uds.* form is used.

Verbs are generally shown as an infinitive, the basic "to" form of the verb: to live, to laugh, to love. An infinitive, whether in Spanish or in English, is the form of the verb before it has been conjugated. Conjugation refers to changing the ending of a verb so it agrees with the subject. Verbs can be regular (most verbs with the same ending follow the same rules) or irregular (there are no rules so you must memorize them).

Regular verbs in Spanish belong to one of three large families—verbs whose infinitives end in *-ar, -er,* or *-ir.* The verbs within each family are conjugated in exactly the same manner. After you've learned the pattern for one family, you know them all.

Subject	-ar verbs (hablar)	-er verbs (comer)	-ir verbs (abrir)
yo	hablo	como	abro
tú	hablas	comes	abres
el, ella, Ud.	habla	come	abre
nosotros	hablamos	comemos	abrimos
vosotros	habláis	coméis	abrís
ellos, ellas, Uds.	hablan	comen	abren

Verb Tables

Tables 2.5, 2.6, and 2.7 provide practical lists of the most frequently used *-ar, -er,* and *-ir* verbs. These are the ones you'll use the most in any given situation.

Table 2.5 Common -ar Verbs

Verb	Pronunciation	Meaning
acompañar	ah-kohm-pah-nyahr	to accompany
alquilar	ahl-kee-lahr	to rent
aterrizar	ah-tehr-ree-sar	to land
ayudar	ah-yoo-dahr	to help
buscar	boos-kahr	to look for
cambiar	kahm-bee-yahr	to change
comprar	kohm-prahr	to buy
desear	deh-seh-yahr	to desire
entrar	ehn-trahr	to enter
escuchar	ehs-koo-chahr	to listen (to)
estudiar	ehs-too-dee-yahr	to study
explicar	ehks-plee-kahr	to explain
firmar	feer-mahr	to sign
hablar	hahb-lahr	to speak, to talk
invitar	een-bee-tahr	to invite
lavar	lah-bahr	to wash
llegar	yeh-gahr	to arrive
mirar	mee-rahr	to look at
necesitar	neh-seh-see-tahr	to need
pagar	pah-gahr	to pay
pasar	pah-sahr	to spend (time)
preguntar	preh-goon-tahr	to ask
presentar	preh-sehn-tahr	to introduce
prestar	prehs-tahr	to lend
regresar	rreh-greh-sahr	to return
reparar	rreh-pah-rahr	to repair
reservar	rreh-sehr-bahr	to reserve
telefonear	teh-leh-foh-neh-yahr	to phone
terminar	tehr-mee-nahr	to end

Verb	Pronunciation	Meaning
tocar	toh-kahr	to touch
tomar	toh-mahr	to take
usar	oo-sahr	to use, to wear
viajar	bee-yah-hahr	to travel

Table 2.6   Common -er Verbs

Verb	Pronunciation	Meaning
aprender	ah-prehn-dehr	to learn
beber	beh-behr	to drink
comer	koh-mehr	to eat
comprender	kohm-prehn-dehr	to understand
creer	kreh-yehr	to believe
deber	deh-behr	to have to, to owe
leer	leh-yehr	to read
responder	rrehs-pohn-dehr	to respond
vender	behn-dehr	to sell

Table 2.7   Common -ir Verbs

Verb	Pronunciation	Meaning
abrir	ah-breer	to open
asistir	ah-sees-teer	to attend
decidir	deh-see-deer	to decide
describir	dehs-kree-beer	to describe
escribir	ehs-kree-beer	to write
recibir	rreh-see-beer	to receive
subir	soo-beer	to go up, to climb
vivir	bee-beer	to live

¡Cuidado!

Verbs ending in *-car*, *-gar*, and *-zar* are regular in the present but irregular in the past tense.

Adjectives at Work

Adjectives help to describe nouns. Unlike in English, in Spanish all adjectives agree in number and gender with the nouns they modify. In other words, in a Spanish sentence, all the words have to match. If the noun is singular, its adjective must also be singular. If the noun is feminine, you must be sure to give the correct feminine form of the adjective.

With most adjectives, you can form the feminine by simply changing the *-o* of the masculine form to an *-a*, as shown in Table 2.8.

Table 2.8   Forming Feminine Adjectives

Masculine	Pronun-ciation	Feminine	Meaning
alto	ahl-toh	alta	tall
bajo	bah-hoh	baja	short
bonito	boh-nee-toh	bonita	pretty
bueno	bweh-noh	buena	good
delicioso	deh-lee-see-yoh-soh	deliciosa	delicious
divertido	dee-behr-tee-doh	divertida	fun
feo	feh-yoh	fea	ugly

Masculine	Pronun-ciation	Feminine	Meaning
flaco	flah-koh	flaca	thin
gordo	gohr-doh	gorda	fat
guapo	gwah-poh	guapa	pretty
magnífico	mahg-nee-fee-koh	magnífica	magnifi-cent
malo	mah-loh	mala	bad
moreno	moh-reh-noh	morena	dark-haired
nuevo	nweh-boh	nueva	new
pequeño	peh-keh-nyoh	pequeña	small
rico	rree-koh	rica	rich
rubio	rroo-bee-yoh	rubia	blond
simpático	seem-pah-tee-koh	simpática	nice
sincero	seen-seh-roh	sincera	sincere
tímido	tee-mee-doh	tímida	shy
viejo	bee-yeh-hoh	vieja	old

The adjectives in Table 2.9 end in *-e*, *-a*, or a consonant. It is not necessary to make any changes to get the feminine form.

Table 2.9   Adjectives

Adjective	Pronunciation	Meaning
Adjectives ending in -e		
alegre	ah-leh-greh	happy
amable	ah-mah-bleh	nice
elegante	eh-leh-gahn-teh	elegant

continues

Table 2.8 (continued)

Adjective	Pronunciation	Meaning
excelente	ehks-seh-lehn-teh	excellent
grande	grahn-deh	big
importante	eem-pohr-tahn-teh	important
inteligente	een-teh-lee-gehn-teh	intelligent
interesante	een-teh-reh-sahn-teh	interesting
pobre	poh-breh	poor
responsable	rrehs-pohn-sah-bleh	responsible
triste	trees-teh	sad
Adjectives ending in -a		
egoísta	eh-goh-ees-tah	selfish
idealista	ee-deh-yah-lees-tah	idealistic
materialista	mah-teh-ree-yah-lees-tah	materialistic
optimista	ohp-tee-mees-tah	optimistic
pesimista	peh-see-mees-tah	pessimistic
realista	rree-yah-lees-tah	realistic
Adjectives ending in a consonant		
cortés	kohr-tehs	courteous
cruel	kroo-ehl	cruel
difícil	dee-fee-seel	difficult
fácil	fah-seel	easy
joven	hoh-behn	young
popular	poh-poo-lahr	popular

In English, adjectives generally are placed before the nouns they modify (for example, the tall man). In Spanish, however, most adjectives come after the nouns the describe (for example, *el hombre grande*).

Don't let this bother you. If you make a mistake, you'll still be understood.

Adverbs in Use

Adverbs are words that describe verbs, adjectives, or other adverbs. In English, most adverbs end in -ly (for example, he dances slowly). In Spanish, they end in *-mente* (for example, *él baila rápidamente*). Adverbs probably will pose few problems as you learn the language.

¡Cuidado!

Masculine adjectives ending in *-or* add an *-a* to form the feminine:

encantador   *encantadora*

Adjectives showing nationality that end in a consonant add *-a* and may drop an accent to form the feminine:

inglés   *inglesa*

Something Extra

If you can't think of the adverb or if the adjective cannot be used with *-mente,* you can use the preposition *con* + a noun:

con cuidado   *cuidadosamente* carefully

con paciencia *pacientemente*   patiently

To form adverbs, simply add *-mente* to the feminine, singular form of the adjective. Remember to look for the letter at the end of the adjective and pay attention to selecting the correct feminine form. Table 2.10 will show you how to do this.

Table 2.10   Adverbs Formed from Feminine Adjectives

Masculine	Feminine	Adverb	Meaning
completo	completa	completamente	completely
especial	especial	especialmente	especially
final	final	finalmente	finally
frecuente	frecuente	frecuentemente	frequently
lento	lenta	lentamente	slowly
rápido	rápida	rápidamente	quickly

Something Extra

When you find it necessary to describe an action with two or more adverbs, add *-mente* only to the last one. The other adverbs should be shown in the feminine, singular adjective form. It is assumed that *-mente* would have been added had they stood alone.

Enrique habla clara, lenta, fácil, y elocuentemente.

Henry speaks clearly, slowly, easily, and eloquently.

Prepositions

Prepositions show the relationship between a noun and another word in a sentence. Table 2.11 shows common prepositions you will find very useful.

Table 2.11   Prepositions

Preposition	Pronunciation	Meaning
a	ah	to, at
además de	ah-deh-mahs deh	in addition to, besides
al lado de	ahl lah-doh deh	at the side of, beside
alrededor (de)	ahl-reh-deh-dohr (deh)	around
antes (de)	ahn-tehs (deh)	before
cerca (de)	sehr-kah (deh)	near
con	kohn	with
contra	kohn-trah	against
de	deh	of, from, about
debajo (de)	deh-bah-hoh (deh)	under
delante (de)	deh-lahn-teh (deh)	in front (of)
dentro (de)	dehn-troh (deh)	within, inside of
después (de)	dehs-pwehs (deh)	after
detrás (de)	deh-trahs (deh)	behind, in back (of)
en	ehn	in
encima (de)	ehn-see-mah (deh)	above
enfrente de	ehn-frehn-teh deh	in front of, opposite, facing
entre	ehn-treh	between, among
en vez de	ehn behs deh	instead of

continues

Table 2.11   (continued)

Preposition	Pronunciation	Meaning
frente a	frehn-teh ah	opposite, facing
fuera de	fweh-rah deh	outside of
hacia	ah-see-yah	toward
hasta	ahs-tah	up to, until
lejos (de)	leh-hohs (deh)	far (from)
para	pah-rah	for, in order to
por	pohr	by, through
según	seh-goon	according to
sin	seen	without
sobre	soh-breh	on, upon

¡Cuidado!

In certain cases, contractions form with the prepositions *a* and *de*, whether they are used alone or as part of a longer expression.

a + el = al   de + el + del
Hablo al *hombre.*   *Hablo* del *hombre.*
I speak *to* the man.   I speak *about* the man.

The following pronouns are used after prepositions:

mí	me	**nosotros(as)**	us
ti	you	**vosotros(as)**	you
él	him	**ellos**	them
ella	her	**ellas**	them
Ud.	you	**Uds.**	you

Chapter 3

Verbs 1-2-3

In This Chapter

- The present
- The present progressive
- The preterit (past tense)
- The imperfect
- The future
- The conditional
- The subjunctive

Since we lead very full, active lives, we always use verbs in a specific tense or time: past, present, or future. We can select a mood: the indicative (expressed in the past, present, or future tense), which states a fact; the imperative or command form; the conditional, which expresses what a subject *would* do under certain conditions; or the subjunctive (expressed in the past, imperfect, or present tense), which expresses wishing, emotion, doubt, need, or necessity. A full understanding of tenses and moods will ensure that you communicate exactly what you are trying to say.

The Present

The present tense is used …

- To express what generally happens in the present:

  Miro la televisión todas las noches.
  I watch television every night.

- To describe or introduce people or events:

  Quiero presentarle a mi hermana menor, Susana.
  I'd like to introduce you to my younger sister, Susan.

- To express events that are taking place:

  Mis amigos van al cine.
  My friends are going to the movies.

- To imply actions or events that will occur in the immediate future:

  Te veo mañana.
  I'll see you tomorrow.

- To express attitudes, feelings, emotions, or opinions:

  ¿Qué piensas de esta oportunidad?
  What do you think of this opportunity?

- To express an action that began in the past and continues in the present:

  Hace un año que estudio el español.
  I've been studying Spanish for a year.

¡Cuidado! _____

The verbs discussed in Chapter 2—those ending in *-ar*, *-er*, and *-ir*—are regular verbs, and all verbs in those families follow the same rules for present tense conjugation. Verbs that have irregular present tense conjugations can be found in Appendix A. They are generally very high-frequency verbs and must be memorized.

Go-go verbs are regular (in all other forms except *yo*) or irregular verbs whose *yo* form ends in *–go* instead of *–o*. The most common go-go verbs are:

- *yo digo*   I say, tell
- *yo hago*   I make, do
- *yo oígo*   I hear
- *yo pongo*   I put
- *yo salgo*   I leave
- *yo tengo*   I have
- *yo traigo*   I bring
- *yo valgo*   I am worth
- *yo vengo*   I come

"Shoe verbs" require a spelling change that works as if we put the subject pronouns that follow one set of rules within the shoe and the others outside the shoe. The shoe looks like this:

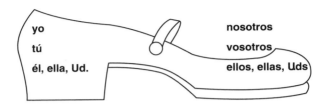

yo	nosotros
tú	vosotros
él, ella, Ud.	ellos, ellas, Uds

Note that these verbs have changes for all subject pronouns except *nosotros* and *vosotros*.

The changes occur as follows:

- Verbs ending in *–ar* and *–er*:

  The vowel in the stem makes the following change:

  e changes to ie

  | pensar (to think) | yo pienso |
  | nosotros pensamos | |

  | querer (to want) | yo quiero |
  | nosotros queremos | |

  o changes to ue

  | mostrar (to show) | yo muestro |
  | nosotros mostramos | |

  | poder (to be able to) | yo puedo |
  | nosotros podemos | |

- Verbs ending in *–ir*:

  The vowel in the stem makes the following change:

  e changes to ie

  | preferir (to prefer) | yo prefiero |
  | nosotros preferimos | |

o changes to ue

dormir (to sleep)   yo d<u>ue</u>rmo
nosotros dormimos

e changes to i

p<u>e</u>dir (to ask)   yo p<u>i</u>do
nosotros pedimos

 Something Extra _____

Verbs ending in *-uir* (but not *-guir*) insert
a *y* after the *u* in all forms within the shoe:

yo incluyo	nosotros incluimos
tú incluyes	vosotros incluís
él incluye	ellos incluyen

Verbs ending in *-iar* and *-uar*, like *guiar* (to
guide), *enviar* (to send), and *variar* (to vary),
require an accent in all forms except
nosotros.

yo envío	nosotros enviamos
tú envías	vosotros enviáis
él envía	ellos envían

Other irregularities appear in Appendix A.

The Present Progressive

The present progressive expresses what a particular
subject is doing right now, at this moment in time.
The present progressive is formed by using the

present tense form of the verb *estar* (to be) that corresponds to the subject. A gerund (the -ing form of the verb) then follows immediately.

Gerunds are formed as follows:

- If the infinitive ends in *–ar*, drop *–ar* and add *–ando*:

  habl**ar** (to speak)   habl**ando**   speaking

  Están hablando español.
  They are speaking Spanish.

- If the infinitive ends in *–er* or *–ir*, drop the respective ending and add *–iendo*:

  beb**er** (to drink)   beb**iendo**   drinking

  Estoy bebiendo té.
  I'm drinking tea.

  escrib**ir** (to write) escrib**iendo**   writing

  ¿Qué estás escribiendo?
  What are you writing?

Something Extra

If an *–er* or *–ir* verb has a stem ending in a vowel, add *–yendo* instead of *–iendo*:

le**er** (to read)   le**y**endo   reading

Está leyendo el periódico.
He's reading the newspaper.

o**ír** (to hear)   o**y**endo   hearing

Estamos oyendo malas noticias.
We're hearing bad news.

The Preterit (The Past Tense)

The preterit expresses an action or event that was begun or completed at a specific time in the past, even if the time isn't mentioned.

> *La película empezó a las ocho.*
> The film began at eight o'clock.

> *Me levanté temprano.*
> I got up early.

The preterit may also express an action or event that was repeated a stated number of times.

> *Fui en España tres veces.*
> I went to Spain three times.

¡Cuidado!

Verbs ending in *-car*, *-gar*, and *-zar* drop the *-ar* infinitive ending to form the preterit and have the following respective spelling changes in the *yo* form only:

c changes to qu	*Yo lo busqué.*	I looked for it.
g changes to gu	*Yo pagué mucho.*	I paid a lot.
z changes to c	*Yo lo gocé.*	I enjoyed it.

To form the preterit of regular verbs, drop the infinitive ending (*-ar, -er, -ir*) and add the endings as illustrated in Table 3.1. Note that regular *-er* and *-ir* verbs have the same preterit endings.

Table 3.1   Forming the Preterit of Regular Verbs

	-ar verbs usar (to use)	-er verbs comer (to eat)	-ir verbs abrir (to open)
yo	usé	comí	abrí
tú	usaste	comiste	abriste
él	usó	comió	abrió
nosotros	usamos	comimos	abrimos
vosotros	usasteis	comisteis	abristeis
ellos	usaron	comieron	abrieron

All irregular Spanish verbs have the same preterit endings regardless of their infinitive endings. These endings are:

yo	*-e*	*nosotros*	*-imos*
tú	*-iste*	*vosotros*	*-isteis*
él	*-o*	*ellos*	*-ieron*

¡Cuidado!

The irregular verbs *ir* (to go) and *ser* (to be) have the same preterit forms:
yo fui, tú fuiste, él fue, nosotros fuimos, vosotros fuisteis, ellos fueron.

High-frequency irregular verbs in the preterit are:

Verb	Stem
andar (to walk)	anduv-
caber (to fit)	cup-

Verb	Stem
estar (to be)	estuv–
hacer (to make, do)	hic-, hiz– (for él, ella, and Ud.)
poder (to be able to)	pud–
querer (to want)	quis–
saber (to know)	sup–
tener (to have)	tuv–
venir (to come)	vin–

¡Cuidado!

The *–ieron* ending for irregular verbs becomes *–eron* before the letter *j*:

decir (to say)	dij–
producir (to produce)	produj–
traer (to bring)	traj–

The Imperfect

The imperfect expresses continuous or repeated actions, events, situations, or states in the past and is used ...

- To describe what *was* or *used to* happen again and again in the past:

  Los niños jugaban.
  The children were playing.

  Todos los sábados yo iba al cine.
  Every Saturday I used to go to the movies.

- To express an ongoing past action:

  Elena trabajaba por la noche.
  Elena worked at night.

- To describe people, things, or time in the past:

  Su madre era muy bonita.
  His mother was very beautiful.

  La calle estaba desierta.
  The street was deserted.

  Eran las cinco de la tarde.
  It was 5 o'clock in the afternoon.

- To express a state of mind in the past with verbs such as *creer* (to believe), *pensar* (to think), *poder* (to be able to), *querer* (to want), and *saber* (to know):

  Ella pensaba ir de compras.
  She was thinking about going shopping.

- To describe a situation that was going on in the past when another action occurred:

  Yo salía cuando el teléfono sonó.
  I was going out when the telephone rang.

To form the imperfect of regular verbs, drop the infinitive ending (-*ar*, -*er*, -*ir*) and add the endings shown in Table 3.2. Note that the imperfect endings are the same for –*er* and –*ir* verbs.

Table 3.2   Forming the Imperfect

	-ar verbs	-er verbs	-ir verbs
yo	-aba	-ía	-ía
tú	-abas	-ías	-ías
él	-aba	-ía	-ía
nosotros	-ábamos	-íamos	-íamos
vosotros	-abais	-íais	-íais
ellos	-aban	-ían	-ían

The three verbs that are irregular in the imperfect are shown in Table 3.3.

Table 3.3   Verbs Irregular in the Imperfect

	ir (to go)	ser (to be)	ver (to see)
yo	iba	era	veía
tú	ibas	eras	veías
él	iba	era	veía
nosotros	íbamos	éramos	veíamos
vosotros	ibais	erais	veíais
ellos	iban	eran	veían

The Future

The future can be expressed in three ways:

- By using the present to imply the future
  Ellos llegan esta noche.
  They are arriving tonight.

- By using *ir* (to go) + *a* + the infinitive of a verb
  Ellos van a llegar esta noche.
  They are going to arrive tonight.
- By using the future tense
  Ellos llegarán esta noche.
  They will arrive tonight.

The future tense is formed by adding the future endings to the infinitive of regular verbs as follows:

yo	*-e*	*nosotros*	*-emos*
tú	*ás*	*vosotros*	*-éis*
él	*-á*	*ellos*	*-án*

Ud. trabajará mañana.
You will work tomorrow.

Yo venderé mi coche pronto.
I will sell my car right away.

Ellos recibirán el paquete.
They will receive the package.

The following verbs have irregular stems in the future and, therefore, do not use the infinitive. To form the future, simply add the ending to the stems indicated:

caber	to fit	cabr-
decir	to say	dir-
hacer	to make	har-
poder	to be able	podr-
poner	to put	pondr-
querer	to want	querr-

saber	to know	sabr-
salir	to leave	saldr-
tener	to have	tendr-
valer	to be worth	valdr-
venir	to come	vendr-

The Conditional

The conditional is a mood that expresses what the subject *would* do or what *would* happen under certain circumstances.

The conditional is formed by adding the *–er* and *–ir* imperfect endings to the future stem of regular and irregular verbs as follows:

yo	-ía	nosotros	-íamos
tú	-ías	vosotros	-íais
él	-ía	ellos	-ían

¿Me hablaría?
Would he speak to me?

Diríamos la verdad.
We would tell the truth.

The Subjunctive

The subjunctive is a mood that expresses wishing, wanting, emotion, doubt, and uncertainty. Since the subjunctive is not a tense (a verb form indicating time), the present subjunctive is used to express actions in the present or future.

The subjunctive is used when the following conditions are met:

- There are two different clauses with two different subjects.
- The two clauses are joined by *que*.
- One of the clauses shows wishing, wanting, emotion, doubt, or uncertainty.

To form the subjunctive of regular verbs, drop the *–o* ending from the *yo* form of the present tense and for *–ar* verbs add the *–er/-ir* present tense verb endings *(-e, -es, -e, -emos, -éis, -en)*, and for *–er/-ir* verbs add the *–ar* present tense verb endings *(-a, -as, -a, -amos, -áis, -an)*.

> *Es importante que te hable.*
> It's important that I speak to you.
>
> *El profesor duda que él aprenda mucho.*
> The teacher doubts that he is learning much.
>
> *Es posible que ellas escriban esta carta.*
> It is possible that they will write this letter.

The following verbs with irregular present tense yo forms will also have irregular subjunctive forms with the *–ar* present tense verb endings:

conocer	to know	conozc-
decir	to say	dig-
hacer	to make, do	hag-
oír	to hear	oig-
poner	to put	pong-

salir	to go out	salg-
traer	to bring	traig-
venir	to come	veng-

¡Cuidado!

In all forms of the subjunctive:

For –*car* verbs, *c* changes to *que*:
yo busque

For –*gar* verbs, *g* changes to *gu*:
nosotros paguemos

For –*zar* verbs, *z* changes to *c*:
ellos crucen

For stem-changing shoe verbs:

- Verbs ending in –*ar* and –*er* have the same stem changes in the subjunctive as they do in the present.

  | *que yo piense* | *que nosotros pensemos* |
  | *que tú vuelvas* | *que vosotros volváis* |

- Verbs ending in –*ir* have the same stem changes in the subjunctive for the *yo*, *tú*, *él*, and *ellos* forms but change the *e* to *i* or *o* to *u* in the *nosotros* and *vosotros* forms.

que él sienta	*que nosotros sintamos*
que yo duerma	*que vosotros durmáis*
que tú pidas	*que nosotros pidamos*

Something Extra

To avoid using the subjunctive, you may use the correctly conjugated form of *tener* + *que* + the infinitive of a verb to express something that has to be done:

I have to work today.

> *Yo tengo que trabajar hoy.*

instead of

> *Es necesario que trabaje hoy.*

High-frequency irregular verbs used in the subjunctive include:

dar (to give): *dé, des, dé, demos, deis, den*

estar (to be): *esté, estés, esté, estemos, estéis, estén*

ir (to go): *vaya, vayas, vaya, vayamos, vayáis, vayan*

saber (to know): *sepa, sepas, sepa, sepamos, sepáis, sepan*

ser (to be): *sea, seas, sea, seamos, seáis, sean*

Chapter 4

Idioms 1-2-3

In This Chapter

- Idiomatically speaking
- Verbal idioms
- Miscellaneous idioms
- Bordering on slang

So what exactly is an idiom? In any language, an *idiom* is a particular word or expression whose meaning cannot be readily understood by either its grammar or the words used to express it. Idioms defy logic but they allow you to speak and express yourself in a foreign language the way a native speaker would. Idioms are acceptable patterns that are part of the standard vocabulary of the language and are listed in bilingual dictionaries.

Idiomatically Speaking

For a better understanding of idioms, take a quick look at some common English idioms that would probably confuse a foreign speaker trying to use the language. Obviously a word-by-word translation would wreak havoc with the intended meaning of these phrases:

- You're driving me crazy!
- I have some time to kill.
- It's raining cats and dogs.
- You'll have to pay through the nose.

Something Extra

Keep handy a list of the idioms you learn in each chapter. Try to use the ones that will be most helpful to you in situations in which you will speak the language.

Verbal Idioms

Some idioms are formed with verbs. To use them, simply conjugate the verb to agree with the subject. Make sure that you put the verb in the proper tense (past, present, future) or mood (conditional, subjunctive).

¡Cuidado!

Hacer is used to describe the weather while *tener* is used to describe the physical condition of a person:

Hace frío.   The weather is cold.

Tiene frío.   He (She) is cold.

acabar de + inf. ah-kah-bahr deh	to have just
contar con kohn-tahr kohn	to rely on
creer que sí (no) kreh-yehr keh see (noh)	to think so (not)
dar a dahr ah	to face
dar un paseo dahr oon pah-seh-yoh	to take a walk
dejar caer deh-hahr kah-yehr	to drop
esperar que sí (no) ehs-peh-rahr keh see (noh)	to hope so (not)
hace + time + past ah-seh	ago
hace buen (mal) tiempo ah-seh bwehn (mahl) tee-yehm-poh	to be nice (bad) weather
hace calor (frío) ah-seh kah-lohr (free-yoh)	to be hot (cold)
hace fresco ah-seh frehs-koh	to be cool
hace sol ah-seh sohl	to be sunny
hacer viento ah-sehr bee-yehn-toh	to be windy

hacer una pregunta ah-sehr oo-nah preh-goon-tah	to ask a question
hacer un viaje ah-sehr oon bee-yah-heh	to take a trip
hacer una visita ah-sehr oo-nah bee-zee-tah	to pay a visit
hacerse tarde ah-sehr-seh tahr-deh	to be getting late
llegar a ser yeh-gahr ah sehr	to become
prestar atención prehs-tahr ah-tehn-see-yohn	to pay attention
querer decir keh-rehr deh-seer	to mean
tardar en tahr-dahr ehn	to delay in
tener___ años teh-nehr ___ ah-nyohs	to be ___ years old
tener calor teh-nehr kah-lohr	to be warm, hot
tener frío teh-nehr free-yoh	to be cold
tener hambre teh-nehr ahm-breh	to be hungry
tener sed teh-nehr sehd	to be thirsty

tener éxito teh-nehr ehk-see-toh	to be successful
tener razón teh-nehr rrah-sohn	to be right
tener sueño teh-nehr sweh-nyoh	to be sleepy
tener cuidado teh-nehr kwee-dah-doh	to be careful
tener prisa teh-nehr pree-sah	to be in a hurry
tener miedo a + noun teh-nehr mee-yeh-doh ah	to be afraid of
tener miedo de + inf. teh-nehr mee-yeh-doh deh	to be afraid to
tener dolor de ___ teh-nehr doh-lohr deh	to have a ___ ache
tener que + inf. teh-nehr keh	to have to
tratar de + inf. trah-tahr deh	to try to
volver a + inf. bohl-behr ah	to (verb) again

Here are some examples showing you how to use these idioms. Note how different subjects, tenses, and moods can be used:

Cuento contigo.	I'm relying on you.
¿Qué quiere decir esto?	What does this mean?

Ellos prestaron atención.   They paid attention.

Es necesario que tengas prisa. You have to hurry.

Miscellaneous Idiomatic Expressions

Many miscellaneous idiomatic expressions begin with prepositions. They generally refer to time, travel, location, and direction. Many idioms allow you to express your opinions and feelings about things. Table 4.1 gives you high-frequency idioms that will certainly come in handy:

Table 4.1 Miscellaneous Idiomatic Expressions

a causa de	ah kow-sah deh	because of
a eso de	ah eso deh	at about
a menudo	ah meh-noo-doh	often
a pesar de	ah peh-sahr deh	in spite of
a tiempo	ah tee-yehm-poh	on time
a veces	ah beh-sehs	at times
a cerca de	ah sehr-kah deh	about, concerning
ahora mismo	ah-oh-rah mees-moh	right now
al + inf.	ahl	upon
al fin	ahl feen	finally
algunas veces	ahl-goo-nahs beh-sehs	sometimes
con mucho gusto	kohn moo-choh goos-toh	gladly
cuanto antes	kwahn-toh ahn-tehs	as soon as possible

de acuerdo	deh ah-kwehr-doh	okay
de esta manera	deh ehs-tah mah-neh-rah	in this way
de memoria	deh meh-moh-ree-yah	by heart
de moda	deh moh-dah	in style
de nada	deh nah-dah	you're welcome
de nuevo	deh nweh-boh	again
de pronto	deh prohn-toh	suddenly
de repente	deh rreh-pehn-teh	suddenly
de vez en cuando	deh behs ehn kwahn-doh	from time to time
dentro de poco	dehn-troh deh poh-koh	shortly, soon
en casa	ehn kah-sah	at home
en lugar de	ehn loo-gahr deh	instead of
en medio de	ehn meh-dee-yoh deh	in the middle of
en punto	ehn poon-toh	exactly
en seguida	ehn seh-gee-dah	immediately
en vez de	ehn behs deh	instead of
es decir	ehs deh-seer	that is to say
hasta luego	ahs-tah lweh-goh	see you later
hoy día	oy dee-yah	nowadays
los (las) dos	lohs (lahs) dohs	both
más tarde	mahs tahr-deh	later
muchas veces	moo-chahs beh-sehs	many times
mucho tiempo	moo-choh tee-yehm-poh	a long time
no importa	noh eem-pohr-tah	it doesn't matter

continues

Table 4.1 (continued)

otra vez	oh-trah behs	again
poco a poco	poh-koh ah poh-koh	little by little
por ejemplo	pohr eh-hehm-ploh	for example
por eso	pohr eh-soh	therefore
por favor	pohr fah-bohr	please
por fin	pohr feen	finally
por lo general	pohr loh heh-neh-rahl	in general
por lo menos	pohr loh meh-nohs	at least
por supuesto	pohr soo-pwehs-toh	of course
qué	keh	how, what, what a
sin duda	seen doo-dah	without a doubt
sin embargo	seen ehm-bahr-goh	however
tal vez	tahl behs	perhaps
todavía no	toh-dah-bee-yah noh	not yet
todo el mundo	toh-doh ehl moon-doh	everybody
ya no	yah noh	no longer

Here are some examples using these idioms:

Viajo en avión.	I'm traveling by plane.
No tenemos mucho tiempo.	We don't have a lot of time.
Repita, por favor.	Please repeat.
¿Vas al cine hoy? Tal vez.	Are you going to the movies today? Perhaps.

Something Extra

Use *¡Qué ...!* to express "how," "what," or "what a" as follows:

How + adjective___!

¡Qué bonito!	How pretty!
¡Qué barbaridad!	How awful!
¡Qué buena suerte!	What good luck!

What (a)___!

¡Qué lástima!	What a pity!
¡Qué buena idea!	What a good idea!
¡Qué mala idea!	What a bad idea!

Bordering on Slang

Slang refers to colorful, popular, informal words or phrases that are not part of the standard vocabulary of the language, but certainly do make it interesting. Considered unconventional, slang has also been commonly referred to as street language. The phrases listed below may be considered mild slang and may come in handy in various situations:

Big deal	*¡No es para tanto!* noh ehs pah-rah tahn-toh
Cut it out!	*¡Déjate de tonterías!* deh-hah-teh deh tohn-teh-ree-yahs

I'm really fed up!	*¡Estoy hasta los pelos con esto!* ehs-toy ahs-tah lohs peh-lohs kohn ehs-toh
I've had it!	*¡Estoy harto de esto!* ehs-toy ahr-toh deh ehs-toh
It goes without saying.	*Dicho está.* dee-choh ehs-tah
It's not worth it.	*¡No vale la pena!* noh bah-leh lah peh-nah
Leave me alone!	*¡Déjame en paz!* deh-hah-meh ehn pahs
Mind your own business!	*¡No te metas donde no te llaman!* noh teh meh-tahs dohn-deh noh teh yah-mahn
Never mind!	*¡Da igual!* dah ee-gwahl
No kidding?	*¿De veras?* deh beh-rahs
No way!	*¡De ninguna manera!* deh neen-goo-nah mah-neh-rah
Of course!	*¡Cómo no!; ¡Claro!* koh-moh noh; klah-roh
Oh no!	*¡Ay, ay, ay!* ah-yee, ah-yee, ah-yee
Shame on you!	*¡Qué vergüenza!* keh behr-goo-wehn-sah

That bothers me!	*¡Eso me fastidia!* eh-soh meh fahs-tee-dee-yah
That infuriates me!	*¡Eso me enfurece!* eh-soh meh ehn-foo-reh-seh
That's going too far!	*¡Es demasiado fuerte!* ehs deh-mah-see-yah-doh fwehr-teh
That's the last straw!	*¡No faltaba más!* noh fahl-tah-bah mahs
The pleasure is mine.	*El gusto es mío.* ehl goos-toh ehs mee-yoh
There's no doubt.	*No hay que darle vueltas.* noh ah-yee keh dahr-leh bwehl-tahs
Wow!	*¡Caramba!* kah-rahm-bah
You bet!	*¡Cómo no!* koh-moh noh
You don't say!	*¡No me digas!* noh meh dee-gahs
You must be kidding!	*¡Qué va!* keh bah
You're driving me nuts!	*¡Me vuelves loco(a)!* meh bwehl-behs loh-koh (kah)

¡Cuidado!

All languages contain idiomatic and slang expressions. That's why it's impossible to translate word-for-word from one language to the next. A better idea is just to try to think of the phrase you want in the language you want.

Chapter 5

All About You

In This Chapter

- Greetings and salutations
- *Ser* versus *estar*
- Professions
- Countries
- Family members
- Possession
- *Tener*
- Asking questions

The best way to learn a foreign language is to find a friend who is a sympathetic native speaker and then just jabber away. Talk about anything and everything that strikes your fancy. Ask to be helped and corrected. Don't be shy about using a dictionary or about asking for help with unfamiliar words. To develop a friendship, you have to talk about yourself and ask about your newfound friend. Don't be shy. Strike up a conversation using some or all of the following phrases as your opening lines:

Spanish	Pronunciation	Meaning
Hola	oh-lah	Hello
Buenos días	bweh-nohs dee-yahs	Good morning
Buenas tardes	bweh-nahs tahr-dehs	Good afternoon
Buenas noches	bweh-nahs noh-chehs	Good evening
Señor	seh-nyohr	Sir
Señorita	seh-nyoh-ree-tah	Miss
Señora	seh-nyoh-rah	Mrs.
Me llamo ...	meh yah-moh	My name is ... (I call myself)
¿Cómo se llama?	koh-moh seh yah-mah	What is your name?
¿Cómo está Ud.?	koh-moh ehs-tah oo-stehd	How are you?
Muy bien	mwee byehn	Very well
Regular	rreh-goo-lahr	So-so
Así, así	ah-see ah-see	So-so
Más o menos	mahs oh meh-nohs	So-so

Most people love to talk about themselves. Engaging in a friendly conversation in which the other person can be the center of attention is always very pleasant. To ask and answer even the simplest questions in Spanish, you need to know the verbs that express "to be"—*ser* and *estar*. These verbs are irregular, and all of their forms must be memorized if you want to use them correctly.

SER

yo soy (soy)	nosotros somos (soh-mohs)
tú eres (eh-rehs)	vosotros sois (soys)
él, ella, Ud. es (ehs)	ellos, ellos, Uds. son (sohn)

1. Expresses origin, nationality, or an inherent characteristic or condition of the subject:

Soy de España.   *Soy americana.*   *Soy alto.*
I'm from Spain.   I'm American.   I'm tall.

2. Identifies a subject or its traits that will probably remain the same for a long period of time:

Mi padre es doctor.   My father is a doctor.

3. Expresses times and dates:

Son las tres.   *Es el tres de mayo.*
It's 3 o'clock.   It's May 3rd.

4. Expresses possession:

Es mi coche.   *Es de Marta.*
It's my car.   It's Martha's.

5. Is used in impersonal expressions:

Es necesario estudiar.   It's necessary to study.

ESTAR

yo estoy (ehs-toy)	nosotros estamos (ehs-tah-mohs)
tú estás (ehs-tahs)	vosotros estáis (ehs-tahys)
él, ella, Ud. está (ehs-tah)	ellos, ellas, Uds. están (ehs-tahn)

continues

1. Expresses a temporary state or quality that will change:

Estoy cansado.   I'm tired.

2. Expresses location:

El hotel está allá.   The hotel is there.

3. Forms the progressive tenses:

Estoy escuchando.   I'm listening.

Something Extra

The present progressive tense is formed as follows:

1. Conjugate the verb *estar* to agree with the intended subject.

2. Use the -ing form of the verb that shows the action. For *-ar* verbs, drop *-ar* from the infinitive and add *-ando*. For *-er* and *-ir* verbs, drop *-er* or *-ir* from the infinitive and add *-iendo*.

Yo estoy cantando.   I am singing.
Estamos comiendo.   We are eating.
Están escribiendo.   They are writing.

And What's Your Line?

Now that you've mastered the verbs *ser* and *estar,* you can easily chat about yourself. Use Table 5.1 to refer to your profession.

Table 5.1   Professions

Profession	Spanish	Pronunciation
accountant	contable (m. or f.)	kohn-tah-bleh
business man	hombre de negocios	ohm-breh deh neh-goh-see-yohs
dentist	dentista (m. or f.)	dehn-tees-tah
doctor	doctor (m.)	dohk-tor
engineer	ingeniero	een-heh-nee-yeh-roh
firefighter	bombero	bohm-beh-roh
government employee	empleado del gobierno	ehm-pleh-yah-doh dehl goh-bee-yehr-noh
hairdresser	barbero	bahr-beh-roh
jeweler	joyero	hoh-yeh-roh
lawyer	abogado	ah-boh-gah-doh
nurse	enfermero	ehn-fehr-meh-roh
police officer	agente de policía (m.)	ah-hen-teh deh poh-lee-see-yah
postal worker	cartero	kahr-teh-roh
programmer	programador	proh-grah-mah-dohr
salesperson	vendedor	behn-deh-dohr
secretary	secretario	seh-kreh-tah-ree-yoh
student	estudiante (m. or f.)	ehs-too-dee-yahn-teh
teacher	profesor	proh-feh-sohr
waiter	camarero	kah-mah-reh-roh
waitress	camarera	kah-mah-reh-rah

¡Cuidado!

To make a profession feminine:

If the profession ends in -o/-or, change the ending to -a.

If the profession ends in -a or -e, no change is necessary.

Where Are You From?

Travelers usually are very curious to know where other travelers come from, especially if they detect a foreign accent. Faraway lands always seem so exotic and exciting, and people love to talk about their hometowns. Use the verb *ser* + *de* + the name of your country to say where you are from. Table 5.2 will help you express yourself quite easily.

Table 5.2   Countries Around the World

Country	Spanish	Pronunciation
Canada	el Canadá	ehl kah-nah-dah
England	Inglaterra	een-glah-teh-rah
France	Francia	frahn-see-yah
Germany	Alemania	ah-leh-mah-nee-yah
Greece	Grecia	greh-see-yah
Ireland	Irlanda	eer-lahn-dah
Italy	Italia	ee-tahl-yah
Japan	el Japón	ehl hah-pohn
Norway	Noruega	nohr-oo-eh-gah
Russia	Rusia	rroo-see-yah

Country	Spanish	Pronunciation
Spain	España	ehs-pah-nyah
Sweden	Suecia	soo-eh-see-yah
Switzerland	Suiza	soo-wee-sah
United States	los Estados Unidos	lohs ehs-tah-dohs oo-nee-dohs

And Now for the Loved Ones

No introductory conversation is complete without opening your wallet and showing photos of those you hold near and dear to your heart. Surprisingly, many people enjoy these corny pictures of your family members. Use Table 5.3 to identify everyone correctly.

Table 5.3   Family Members

Member	Pronunciation	Meaning
abuelo	ah-bweh-loh	grandfather
abuela	ah-bweh-lah	grandmother
padrino	pah-dree-noh	godfather
padrina	pah-dree-nah	godmother
padre	pah-dreh	father
madre	mah-dreh	mother
padastro	pah-dahs-troh	stepfather
madastra	mah-dahs-trah	stepmother
hijo	ee-hoh	son, child
hija	ee-hah	daughter
hermano	ehr-mah-noh	brother

continues

Table 5.3 (continued)

Member	Pronunciation	Meaning
hermana	ehr-mah-nah	sister
hermanastro	ehr-mah-nahs-troh	stepbrother
hermanastra	ehr-mah-nahs-trah	stepsister
primo	pree-moh	cousin
prima	pree-mah	cousin (female)
sobrino	soh-bree-noh	nephew
sobrina	soh-bree-nah	niece
tío	tee-yoh	uncle
tía	tee-yah	aunt
nieto	nee-yeh-toh	grandson
nieta	nee-yeh-tah	granddaughter
suegro	sweh-groh	father-in-law
suegra	sweh-grah	mother-in-law
yerno	yehr-noh	son-in-law
nuera	nweh-rah	daughter-in-law
cuñado	koo-nyah-doh	brother-in-law
cuñada	koo-nyah-dah	sister-in-law
novio	noh-bee-yoh	boyfriend
novia	noh-bee-yah	girlfriend

Here are some useful plurals and their spellings:

Table 5.4 Plurals of Family Names

Member	Pronunciation	Meaning
hijos	ee-hohs	children
padres	pah-drehs	parents
abuelos	ah-bweh-lohs	grandparents

Member	Pronunciation	Meaning
suegros	sweh-grohs	in-laws
parientes	pah-ree-yehn-tehs	relatives
padrinos	pah-dree-nohs	godparents

You Belong to Me

To show possession in English, we use 's or s' after a noun. There are no apostrophes in Spanish, however. To translate "Julio's mother" into Spanish, a speaker would have to say "the mother of Julio," which is "*la madre de Julio.*" The preposition *de* means of and is used to express possession or relationship.

Possessive adjectives also can be used to show possession, as shown in Table 5.5. A possessive adjective should agree with the item possessed not the possessor.

Es mi tía.   *Son mis hijos.*
That's my aunt.   They are my sons.

Table 5.5   Possessive Adjectives

Used Before Masculine Nouns		Used Before Feminine Nouns		
Singular	Plural	Singular	Plural	English
mi	mis	mi	mis	my
tu	tus	tu	tus	your
su	sus	su	sus	his, her, your, its
nuestro	nuestros	nuestra	nuestras	our
vuestro	vuestros	vuestra	vuestras	your
su	sus	su	sus	their

This Is What I Have

Perhaps you would like to discuss how many children you have or your age. You also might want to tell how you feel at a particular moment. The verb you will find most helpful in these situations is *tener* (to have). Like the verbs *ser* and *estar*, *tener* is an irregular verb. All its forms (as seen in Table 5.6) must be memorized.

Table 5.6   Conjugating Tener (to Have)

Conjugated Form of Tener	Pronunciation	Meaning
yo tengo	tehn-goh	I have
tú tienes	tee-yeh-nehs	You have
él, ella, Ud. tiene	tee-yeh-neh	He, she, one has
nosotros tenemos	teh-neh-mohs	We have
vosotros tenéis	teh-neh-yees	You have
ellos, ellas, Uds. tienan	tee-yeh-nehn	They have

Idioms with Tener

The idiomatic expressions in Table 5.7 are used quite frequently in everyday conversation. Make sure to conjugate the verb when you use it in context:

> *Yo tengo veinte años.*   I'm 20 years old.

Table 5.7   Idioms with Tener

Idiom	Pronunciation	Expression
tener calor	teh-nehr kah-lohr	to be hot
tener dolor de	teh-nehr doh-lohr deh	to have an ache in

Idiom	Pronunciation	Expression
tener frío	teh-nehr free-yoh	to be cold
tener ganas de + infinitive	teh-nehr gah-nahs deh	to feel like
tener hambre	teh-nehr ahm-breh	to be hungry
tener miedo de	teh-nehr mee-yeh-doh deh	to be afraid of
tener que + infinitive	teh-nehr keh	to have to
tener razón	teh-nehr rrah-sohn	to be right
tener sed	teh-nehr sehd	to be thirsty
tener sueño	teh-nehr sweh-nyoh	to be sleepy
tener … años	teh-nehr ah-nyohs	to be … years old

Asking Questions

If your Spanish is not quite as perfect as you'd like, you'll probably be content to ask people simple yes or no questions. Besides, that way you won't look too nosy.

Intonation

The easiest way to show that you are asking a question is simply to change your intonation by raising your voice at the end of the sentence.

> *¿Eres americano?*
> Are you American?

¡Cuidado!

In Spanish, put an upside down question mark at the beginning of the question and a standard one at the end.

Tags

Another simple way to ask a question is to add a tag such as *¿verdad?*, *¿no?*, or *¿está bien?* to the end of a statement. These tags can mean "really?," "isn't that so?," "is it?," "isn't it?," "are you?," "aren't you?," "do you?," "don't you?," "all right?," or "okay?"

> *Eres americano, ¿verdad? (¿no?, ¿está bien?)*
>
> You're American, right? (isn't that so?, aren't you?)

Inversion

Inversion means reversing the word order of the subject pronoun and the conjugated verb form.

> *¿Eres tú americano?*

Getting the Scoop

If you're anything like me, a simple yes or no answer never suffices. Use the questions in Table 5.8 to get all the information you want.

Table 5.8   Information Questions

Word/Phrase	Pronunciation	Meaning
adónde	ah-dohn-deh	to where
a qué hora	ah keh oh-rah	at what time
a quién	ah kee-yehn	to whom
a qué	ah keh	to what
con quién	kohn kee-yehn	with whom
con qué	kohn keh	with what
cuál	kwahl	which
de quién	deh kee-yehn	of, about, from whom
de qué	deh keh	of, about, from what
cuánto	kwahn-toh	how much, many
cómo	koh-moh	how
dónde	dohn-deh	where
de dónde	deh dohn-deh	from where
por qué	pohr keh	why
cuándo	kwahn-doh	when
quién	kee-yehn	who, whom
qué	keh	what

The easiest way to ask for information is to put the question word immediately before the verbal phrase or thought.

> *¿**Con quién** viaja Ud.?*   With whom are you traveling?

¿Qué? asks "what?" when referring to a description, a definition, or an explanation and asks "which?" when used before a noun.

¿Qué es esto?	What's that?
¿Qué estás comiendo?	What are you eating?
¿Qué programa estás mirando?	Which program are you watching?

¿Cuál? and *¿Cuáles?* generaly ask "which?" They ask "what?" before the verb *ser* (to be), except when asking for the definition of a word (when *¿qué?* is used). They ask "which (one)?" before the preposition *de*.

¿Cuál es su nombre? What's your name?	*¿Cuáles quieres?* Which (ones) do you want?
¿Cuál de los dos prefieres?	Which (one) of the two do you prefer?

In Spanish, all words that ask questions have accent marks. This distinguishes them from words that are spelled the same but that state information rather than asking for it.

¿Dónde vives? Where do you live?	*Yo no sé donde tú vives.* I don't know where you live.

Something Extra

When followed by a noun, *cuánto* is used as an adjective and must agree in number and gender with the noun:

¿Cuánto dinero tienes?
How much money do you have?

¿Cuántas muchachas están cantando?
How many girls are singing?

Chapter 6

Navigating the Airport

In This Chapter

- On the airplane and in the airport
- All about *ir* (to go)
- Giving and receiving directions
- What to say when you don't understand

So you're planning a trip by plane. Be sure to shop around and compare prices for your ticket. A non-refundable ticket isn't a bargain if you have to change your plans midstream.

Many people are all too well aware that a plane ride can be long and tedious. At times, you might experience minor inconveniences or delays for a wide variety of reasons. During your trip, you might want to change your seat or perhaps ask the flight crew some typical tourist questions. No doubt, if you are traveling on a foreign airline, you might find it helpful to use your knowledge of the language to help you get all the information you need. The terms in Table 6.1 will help you face any problem you might have.

Table 6.1 On the Inside

In-Plane Term	Spanish	Pronunciation
aisle	el pasillo	ehl pah-see-yoh
to board	abordar	ah-bohr-dahr
by the window	cerca de la ventana	sehr-kah deh lah behn-tah-nah
crew	el equipo	ehl eh-kee-poh
to deplane, to exit	salir	sah-leer
emergency exit	la salida de emergencia	lah sah-lee-dah deh eh-mehr-hehn-see-yah
gate	la salida	lah sah-lee-dah
landing	el aterrizaje	ehl ah-teh-rree-sah-heh
life vest	el chaleco salvavidas	ehl chah-leh-koh sahl-bah-bee-dahs
(non) smokers	(no) fumadores	(noh) foo-mah-doh-rehs
on the aisle	en el pasillo	ehn ehl pah-see-yoh
row	la fila	lah fee-lah
seat	el asiento	ehl ah-see-yehn-toh
seat belt	el cinturón de seguridad	ehl seen-too-rohn deh seh-goo-ree-dahd
to smoke	fumar	foo-mahr
take off	el despegue	ehl dehs-peh-geh
trip	el viaje	ehl bee-yah-heh

The Eagle Has Landed

After you've landed, there should be plenty of signs to point you in the right direction. Where should you go first? You know it will take your bags a while to be unloaded. Do you need to use the bathroom? How about some foreign currency? After a delicious airline repast, do you still crave something to eat? Table 6.2 provides all the words you need to know once you are inside the airport.

Table 6.2   At the Airport

Place	Spanish	Pronunciation
airline	la aerolínea	lah ah-eh-roh-lee-neh-yah
airplane	el avión	ehl ah-bee-yohn
airport	el aeropuerto	ehl ah-eh-roh-pwehr-toh
arrival	la llegada	lah yeh-gah-dah
baggage claim area	el reclamo de equipaje	ehl rreh-klah-moh deh eh-kee-pah-heh
bathrooms	los baños	lohs bah-nyohs
bus stop	la parada de deh autobús	lah pah-rah-dah ow-toh-boos
car rental	el alquiler de carros	ehl ahl-kee-lehr deh kah-rrohs
cart	el carrito	ehl kah-rree-toh
counter	el mostrador	ehl mohs-trah-dohr
customs	la aduana	lah ah-dwah-nah
departure	la salida	lah sah-lee-dah
elevators	los ascensores	lohs ah-sehn-soh-rehs
entrance	la entrada	lah ehn-trah-dah

continues

Table 6.2 (continued)

Place	Spanish	Pronunciation
exit	la salida	lah sah-lee-dah
flight	el vuelo	ehl bweh-loh
gate	la puerta	lah pwehr-tah
information	la informaciónes	lah een-fohr-mah-see-yoh-nehs
lost and found	la oficina de objetos perdidos	lah oh-fee-see-nah deh ohb-heh-tohs pehr-dee-dohs
to miss the flight	perder el vuelo	pehr-dehr ehl bweh-loh
money exchange	el cambio de dinero	ehl kahm-bee-yoh deh dee-neh-roh
porter	el portero	ehl pohr-teh-roh
stop-over	la escala	lah ehs-kah-lah
suitcase	la maleta	lah mah-leh-tah
ticket	el boleto	ehl boh-leh-toh

Where Are You Going?

It's easy to get lost in sprawling international airports. To get yourself back on track, you need to know how to ask the correct questions. The following question will help you the most:

> *¿Dónde está* + singular noun?
> *¿Dónde están* + plural noun?
> *¿Dónde está la salida?*   *¿Dónde están los baños?*
> Where's the exit?   Where are the bathrooms?

One verb that will really come in handy is shown in Table 6.3. *Ir* (to go) is an irregular verb that must be memorized.

Table 6.3   Conjugating Ir (to Go)

Conjugated Form of Ir	Pronunciation	Meaning
yo voy	boy	I go
tú vas	bahs	you go
él, ella, Ud. va	bah	he, she, one goes
nosotros vamos	bah-mohs	we go
vosotros vais	bahys	you go
ellos, ellas, Uds. van	bahn	they go

 Something Extra

Use *ir* + *a* to express going to a city, state, or country, as follows:

> *Voy a Nueva York.*
> I'm going to New York.

Use *ir* + *en* to express the many different ways to go someplace, as follows:

> *Voy a Nueva York en avión*
> I'm going to New York by plane.

Note the exception: *a pie*, on foot.

> *Voy al cine a pie.*
> I'm walking (going on foot) to the movies.

Complications

If the place you want to go is not within pointing distance, you'll need other directions. The verbs in Table 6.4 can help you get where you want to go or can help you aid someone else who is lost.

¡Cuidado!

Use either *Ud.* (singular) or *Uds.* (plural) as the subject of your command. These are the easiest forms to master. You can use the subject pronoun after the verb. To make the command negative, simply put no before the verb.

Tome (Ud.) el coche.   Take the car.

No crucen (Uds.)   Don't cross the
la calle.   street.

Table 6.4   Giving Directions

Verb	Pronunciation	Meaning
baje(n)	bah-heh(n)	go down
camine(n)	kah-mee-neh(n)	walk
continue(n)	kohn-tee-noo-weh(n)	continue
cruce(n)	kroo-seh(n)	cross
doble(n)	doh-bleh(n)	turn
pase(n)	pah-seh(n)	pass
sea(n)	seh-yah(n)	be
siga(n)	seh-gah(n)	follow, continue

Verb	Pronunciation	Meaning
suba(n)	soo-bah(n)	go up
tenga(n)	tehn-gah(n)	have
tome(n)	toh-meh(n)	take
vaya(n)	bah-yah(n)	go

Por Versus Para

The Spanish words *por* and *para* can both mean "for." Consequently, there is often much confusion about when to use each. You should keep in mind the following rules:

Por Indicates	Para Indicates
motion	**destination to a place**
Paso por *la salida.*	*El avión sale* para *Cuba.*
I pass by the exit.	The airplane leaves for Cuba.
means, manner	**destination to a recipient**
Viajo por *taxi.*	*Este regalo es* para *mi amigo.*
I travel by taxi.	This gift is for my friend.
a period of time	**a time limit**
Duermo por *la noche.*	*La cita es* para *el martes.*
I sleep at night.	The appointment is for Tuesday.
frequency, in exchange for	**purpose**
Salgo una vez por *mes.*	*Es un billete* para *el tren.*
I go out once a month.	It's a ticket for the train.
Son dos plumas por *$20.*	
They are two pens for $20.	

What Did You Say?

What if someone gives you directions and you don't understand? Perhaps the person with whom you are speaking is mumbling, is speaking too fast, has a strong accent, or uses words you don't know. Don't be embarrassed. The phrases in Table 6.5 can be a valuable aid if you need to have something repeated or if you need more information.

Table 6.5   When You Don't Understand

Expression	Pronunciation	Meaning
Con permiso	kohn pehr-mee-soh	Excuse me
Perdóneme	pehr-doh-neh-meh	Excuse me
Yo no comprendo	yoh noh kohm-prehn-doh	I don't understand
Yo no entiendo	yoh noh ehn-tee-yehn-doh	I don't understand
Yo no te oigo	yoh noh teh oy-goh	I don't hear you
Repita por favor	rreh-pee-tah pohr fah-bohr	Please repeat it
Otra vez	oh-trah behs	One more time/again
Hable más despacio	hah-bleh mahs dehs-pah-see-yoh	Speak more slowly
¿Qué dijo?	keh dee-hoh	What did you say?

Getting to Your Destination

In This Chapter

- Means of transportation
- Cardinal numbers
- Telling time
- Time expressions

If you're traveling in a Spanish-speaking country, several different means of transportation can get you to your destination. Consider the following: Are you traveling light? If so, you might want to mingle with people and take buses, subways, and trains. How tight is your budget and how much time do you have? If money is no object or if you're in a hurry, a taxi might be your best option. Do you enjoy seeing the countryside? If you're confident and are familiar with traffic laws and street signs, you might just want to rent a car.

Here's how to say how you're getting there:

Yo tomo … (yoh toh-moh)   I'm taking …

English	Spanish	Pronunciation
the boat	el barco	ehl bahr-koh
the bus	el autobús	ehl ow-toh-boos
the car	el coche	ehl koh-cheh
the car	el automóvil	ehl ow-toh-moh-beel
the car	el carro	ehl kah-rroh
the subway	el metro	ehl meh-troh
the taxi	el taxi	ehl tahk-see
the train	el tren	ehl trehn

If You're Traveling by Bus

The bus system in Madrid is efficient and inexpensive. A bus stop (*una parada de autobús*) is clearly marked by numbers. Transfers are not free (but bus service is quite inexpensive). Buses don't stop automatically; they must be hailed. A free bus map (*un plano de la red*) can easily be obtained at major tourist attractions and hotels.

In Mexico City the buses tend to be very crowded and are more expensive than the subway. The routes go all over town and tend to be confusing.

Where is the nearest bus stop?
¿Dónde está la parada de autobús más cercana?
dohn-deh ehs-tah lah pah-rah-dah deh ow-toh-boos mahs sehr-kah-nah

How much is the fare?
¿Cuánto cuesta el billete?
kwahn-toh kwehs-tah ehl bee-yeh-teh

Do I need exact change?
¿Necesito cambio exacto?
neh-seh-see-toh kahm-bee-yoh ehk-sahk-toh

If You're Traveling by Subway

The subway systems in Madrid and Barcelona can
boast of their cleanliness, comfort, safety, and econ-
omy. The 11 metro lines in Madrid are easily distin-
guishable on maps by numbers and different colors.
Un plan del metro, a subway map, can be conveniently
obtained for free at metro stops, hotels, department
stores, and tourist offices. The sign *"Correspondencia"*
indicates that free transfers and connections are
available. If you don't exit, you can transfer as often
as you like on just one ticket. Navigating the metro
is easy—just look at the name of the last stop in the
direction you want to go and then follow the signs
indicating that station.

Buenos Aires and Mexico City also have very clean
and efficient subway systems.

Where is the nearest subway?
¿Dónde está la estación de metro más cercana?
dohn-deh ehs-tah lah ehs-tah-see-yohn deh
meh-troh mahs sehr-kah-nah

Where can I buy a ticket?
¿Dónde puedo comprar un billete?
dohn-deh pweh-doh kohm-prahr oon bee-yeh-teh

How much is the fare?
¿Cuánto es la tarifa?
kwahn-toh ehs lah tah-ree-fah

How many more stops are there?
¿Hay cuántas paradas más?
ahy kwahn-tahs pah-rah-dahs mahs

What's the next station?
¿Cuál es la prómixa estación?
kwahl ehs lah prohk-see-mah ehs-tah-see-yohn

Where is there a map?
¿Dónde hay un mapa?
dohn-deh ahy oon mah-pah

If You're Traveling by Taxi

Always try to take a metered taxi so you know exactly what fare to expect. Surcharges are imposed for luggage and night and holiday fares. *Un gran turismo* is an unmetered public-service taxi that charges higher rates. Remember to ask for the fare in advance if this is your choice. In Mexico City, orange-colored taxis generally are privately owned and can be called in advance; yellow cabs cruise for passengers. *Un colectivo* is a van or car that can be shared with other travelers going in the same general direction.

Where is the nearest taxi stand?
¿Dónde está la parada de taxi más cercana?
dohn-deh ehs-tah lah pah-rah-dah deh tahk-see mahs sehr-kah-nah

Would you please call me a cab?
¿Puede Ud. conseguirme un taxi, por favor?
pweh-deh oo-stehd kohn-seh-geer-meh oon tahk-see pohr fah-bohr

I want to go …
Quiero ir …
kee-yeh-roh eer

Stop here.
Pare aquí.
pah-reh ah-kee

How much is it to …
¿Cuánto cuesta hasta …
kwahn-toh kwehs-tah ahs-tah …

Wait for me.
Espéreme.
ehs-peh-reh-meh

If You're Going by Train

If you're visiting Spain, Red Nacional de Ferrocar-
riles Españoles (RENFRE) is the national railroad
network of the country and is comparable to
AMTRAK in the United States. Spain has the most
inexpensive train fare in Europe. American travelers
can purchase a Eurail Pass, which permits unlimited
travel rights. The price of this card varies according
to the number of travel days you choose: 15, 25, 40,
60, or 90.

Where is the nearest train station?
¿Dónde está la estacíon de tren más cercana?
dohn-deh ehs-tah lah ehs-tah-see-yohn deh
trehn mahs sehr-kah-nah

I would like …
Quisiera …
kee-see-yeh-rah

a first (second) class ticket.
un billete de primera (segunda) clase.
oon bee-yeh-teh deh pree-meh-rah
(seh-goon-dah) klah-seh

a round-trip ticket.
un billete de ida y vuelta.
oon bee-yeh-teh deh ee-dah ee bwehl-tah

a (non) smoking compartment.
un departamento para (no) fumadores.
oon deh-pahr-tah-mehn-toh pah-rah (noh)
foo-mah-doh-rehs

Is it a local (express)?
¿Es un tren local (un rápido)?
ehs oon trehn loh-kahl (oon rrah-pee-doh)

From what platform does it leave?
¿De qué andén sale?
deh keh ahn-dehn sah-leh

If You're Traveling by Car

So you're daring enough to go to *un alquiler de coches*
to rent a car. Good for you! Always compare rates
before you make a final choice. Don't be surprised
when the price at the gas pump is almost double
what you generally pay back home.

I'd like to rent a (give make of car).
Quiero alquilar un _____.
kee-yeh-roh ahl-kee-lahr oon _____

I prefer automatic transmission.
Prefiero el cambio automático.
preh-fee-yeh-roh ehl kahm-bee-yoh ow-toh-mah-
tee-koh

How much does it cost per day (per week) (per kilometer)?
¿Cuánto cuesta por día (por semana) (por kilómetro)?
kwahn-toh kwehs-tah pohr dee-yah (pohr seh-mah-nah) (por kee-loh-meh-troh)

How much is the insurance?
¿Cuánto es el seguro?
kwahn-toh ehs ehl seh-goo-roh

Is the gas included?
¿Está incluída la gasolina?
ehs-tah een-kloo-eee-dah lah gah-soh-lee-nah

Do you accept credit cards? Which ones?
¿Acepta Ud. tarjetas de crédito? ¿Cuáles?
ahk-sehp-tah oo-stehd tahr-heh-tahs deh kreh-dee-toh kwah-lehs

Do you fill it up with gas?
¿Lo llena Ud. con gasolina?
loh yeh-nah oo-stehd kohn gah-soh-lee-nah

¡Cuidado!

If you decide to rent a car, open the trunk and make sure there is a jack—*un gato* (oon gah-toh)—and a spare tire—*una goma de repuesto* (oo-nah goh-mah deh rrehs-pwehs-toh).

In Europe, distance is measured in kilometers. Table 7.1 shows the approximate equivalents.

Table 7.1 Distance Measures (Approximate)

Miles	Kilometers
.62	1
3	5
6	10
12	20
31	50
62	100

Heading in the Right Direction

By all means, learn your destination's road signs—some are not as obvious as they should be. You also need to know your compass directions.

Meaning	Direction	Pronunciation
to the North	al norte	ahl nohr-teh
to the East	al este	ahl ehs-teh
to the South	al sur	ahl soor
to the West	al oeste	ahl oh-wehs-teh

Familiarize yourself with the following before you venture out on your own in car.

What's Your Number?

To tell someone which flight or bus you are taking or to figure out how much a rental car is going to set you back, you need to learn the Spanish numbers listed in Table 7.2. Believe it or not, these very same numbers will come in handy when you want to tell time, to count money, or to reveal your age.

Table 7.2   Cardinal Numbers

No.	Spanish	Pronunciation	No.	Spanish	Pronunciation
0	cero	seh-roh	3	tres	trehs
1	uno	oo-noh	4	cuatro	kwah-troh
2	dos	dohs	5	cinco	seen-koh

continues

Table 7.2 (continued)

No.	Spanish	Pronun-ciation	No.	Spanish	Pronun-ciation
6	seis	seh-yees	40	cuarenta	kwah-rehn-tah
7	siete	see-yeh-teh	50	cincuenta	seen-kwehntah
8	ocho	oh-choh	60	sesenta	seh-sehn-tah
9	nueve	noo-weh-beh	70	setenta	seh-tehn-tah
10	diez	dee-yehs	80	ochenta	oh-chen-tah
11	once	ohn-seh	90	noventa	noh-behn-tah
12	doce	doh-seh	100	ciento	see-yehn-toh
13	trece	treh-seh	101	ciento uno	see-yehn-toh oo-noh
14	catorce	kah-tohr-seh	200	dos-cientos	dohs-see-yehn-tohs
15	quince	keen-seh	500	quini-entos	kee-nee-yehn-tohs
16	diez y seis	dee-yehs ee seh-yees	700	seteci-entos	seh-teh-see-yehn-tohs
17	diez y siete	dee-yehs ee see-yeh-teh	900	noveci-entos	noh-beh-see-yehn-tohs
18	diez y ocho	dee-yehs ee oh-choh	1000	mil	meel
19	diez y nueve	dee-yehs ee noo-eh-beh	2000	dos mil	dohs meel
20	veinte	behn-teh	100,000	cien mil	see-yehn meel
21	veinti-uno	behn-tee-oo-noh	1,000,000	un mil-lión	oon meel-yohn
22	veinti-dós	behn-tee-dohs	2,000,000	dos mil-liones	dohs meel-yoh-nehs
30	treinta	trehn-tah			

Something Extra

The Spanish write the number 1 with a little hook on top. To distinguish a 1 from a 7, they put a line through the 7, as in 7̸.

In numerals and decimals, wherever we use commas, the Spanish use periods (and vice versa).

English	Spanish
1,000	1.000
.25	0,25
$9.95	$9,95

Spanish numbers are not too tricky. Look carefully again at Table 7.2, however, to pick up the following pointers:

- The conjunction *y* (and) is used only for numbers between 16 and 99.

- *Uno* is used only when counting. It becomes *un* before a masculine noun and *una* before a feminine noun.

  uno, dos, tres …
  one, two, three

  treinta y un muchachos
  thirty-one boys

  un hombre y una mujer
  a man and woman

  veinte y una muchachas
  twenty-one girls

- The numbers 16–19 and 21–29 are generally written as one word. When this is done, the numbers 16, 22, 23, and 26 have accents:

16	*dieciséis*	22	*veintidós*
17	*diecisiete*	23	*veintitrés*
21	*veintiuno*	26	*veintiséis*

- Compounds of *ciento* (*doscientos, trescintos*) should agree with a feminine noun.

doscientos hombres	two hundred men
trescientas mujeres	three hundred women

- *Ciento* becomes *cien* before nouns and before the numbers *mil* and *millones*. Before all other numbers, *ciento* is used.

cien libros	one hundred books
cien mil personas	one hundred thousand people
ciento veinte carros	one hundred twenty cars
cien millones de dólares	one billion dollars

- Although it is not used before *ciento* or *mil, un* is used before *millón*. If a noun follows *millón*, put *de* between *millón* and the noun.

ciento pesetas	100 pesetas
un millón de habitantes	1,000,000 inhabitants
mil quinientos años	1,500 years

Do You Have the Time?

Now that you have the hang of Spanish numbers, it should be rather easy to express the time, as explained in Table 7.3.

What time is it?   At what time?
¿Qué hora es?   *¿A qué hora?*
keh oh-rah ehs   ah keh oh-rah

Table 7.3   Time

English	Spanish	Pronunciation
It is 1:00.	Es la una.	ehs lah oo-nah
It is 2:05.	Son las dos y cinco.	sohn lahs dohs ee see-koh
It is 3:10.	Son las tres y diez.	sohn lahs trehs y dee-yehs
It is 4:15.	Son las cuatro y cuarto.	sohn lahs kwah-troh ee kwahr-toh
It is 5:20.	Son las cinco y veinte.	sohn lahs see-koh ee behn-teh
It is 6:25.	Son las seis y veinticinco.	sohn lahs seh-yees ee behn-tee-seen-koh
It is 7:30.	Son las siete y media.	sohn lahs see-yeh-teh ee meh-dee-yah
It is 7:35 (25 min. to 8).	Son las ocho menos veinte y cinco.	sohn lahs oh-choh meh-nohs behn-teh-seen-koh
It is 8:40 (20 min. to 9).	Son las nueve menos veinte.	sohn lahs noo-weh-beh meh-nohs behn-teh
It is 9:45 (15 min. to 10).	Son las diez menos cuarto.	sohn lahs dee-yehs meh-nohs kwahr-toh
It is 10:50 (10 min. to 11).	Son las once menos diez.	sohn lahs ohn-seh meh-nohs dee-yehs
It is 11:55 (5 min. to 12).	Son las doce menos cinco.	sohn lahns doh-seh meh-nohs seen-koh

continues

Table 7.3   (continued)

English	Spanish	Pronunciation
It is noon.	Es el mediodía.	ehs ehl meh-dee-yoh-dee-yah
It is midnight.	Es la media-noche.	ehs lah meh-dee-yah-noh-cheh

When telling time make sure you do the following:

- Use *es* for "it is" when saying it is 1 o'clock. Use *son* for other numbers because they are plural.

- Use the hour + *y* + the number of minutes to express the time after the hour.

- Use the following hour + *menos* + the number of minutes before that hour whenever it is more than half past the hour.

  Son las tres menos cuarto.
  It's 2:45.

  It also is not unusual to hear the time expressed as follows:

  Son las dos y cuarenta y cinco.
  It's 2:45.

It's not enough to know how to say what the time is. You might want to know at what time an activity is planned or whether it is taking place in the morning, the afternoon, or the evening. The expressions in Table 7.4 will help you deal with time.

Table 7.4   Time Expressions

Expression	Spanish	Pronunciation
a second	un segundo	oon seh-goon-doh
a minute	un minuto	oon mee-noo-toh
an hour	una hora	oo-nah oh-rah
in the morning (A.M.)	de la mañana	deh lah mah-nyah-nah
in the afternoon (P.M.)	de la tarde	deh lah tahr-deh
in the evening (P.M.)	de la noche	deh lah noh-cheh
at what time	a qué hora	ah keh oh-rah
at exactly 1:00	a la una en punto	ah lah oo-nah ehn poon-toh
at exactly 2:00	a las dos en punto	ah lahs dohs ehn poon-toh
at about 2:00	a eso de las dos	ah eh-soh deh lahs dohs
a quarter of an hour	un cuarto de hora	oon kwahr-toh deh oh-rah
a half hour	una media hora	oo-nah meh-dee-yah oh-rah
in an hour	en una hora	ehn oo-nah oh-rah
until 2:00	hasta las dos	ahs-tah lahs dohs
before 3:00	antes de las tres	ahn-tehs deh lahs trehs
after 3:00	después de las tres	dehs-pwehs deh lahs trehs
since what time	desde qué hora	dehs-deh keh oh-rah
since 6:00	desde las seis	dehs-deh lahs seh-yees
an hour ago	hace una hora	ah-seh oo-nah oh-rah
per hour	por hora	pohr oh-rah

continues

Table 7.4 (continued)

Expression	Spanish	Pronunciation
early	temprano	tehm-prah-noh
late	tarde	tahr-deh
late (in arriving)	en retraso	ehn rreh-trah-soh
on time	a tiempo	ah tee-yehm-poh
see you later	hasta luego	ahs-tah loo-weh-goh
see you soon	hasta la vista	ahs-tah lah bees-tah
see you tomorrow	hasta mañana	ahs-tah mah-nyah-nah
good-bye	adiós	ah-dee-yohs

Chapter 8

A Hospitable Hotel

In This Chapter

- Getting the best from your hotel
- Ordinal numbers

No matter where you go in the Spanish-speaking world, a U.S. travel agent can help you find accommodations and make reservations that suit both your needs and your budget. For the more adventurous traveler, it might prove more economical to bargain for a room rate in Mexico or in rural areas throughout the Spanish-speaking world.

Hotel Accomodations

If you plan to stay in a Spanish-speaking country, possible accommodations include:

- *Un hotel* (oon oh-tehl): You can find conveniently located hotel rooms to fit every budget. You're best to make advance reservations, especially when traveling during a location's peak travel times. Hotels are usually rated by the government or a travel-rating organization using a star system ranging from inexpensive (one star) to very expensive (five stars). Every hotel has an outside plaque indicating an H for hotel.

- *Una pensión* (oo-nah pehn-see-yohn): This accommodation is similar to a rooming house, where guests pay for a room and all or part of their meals. These establishments are quite popular throughout Europe.

- *Un albergue* (oon ahl-behr-goo-weh): This lodging is a small, modest inn generally found in rural areas. *Los albergues juveniles* (lohs ahl-behr-gwehs hoo-beh-nee-lehs) are youth hostels that are similar to college dormitories, generally with separate facilities for males and females. Because they are so inexpensive, they are extremely popular with the backpacking crowd.

- *Un parador* (oon pah-rah-dohr): Some former royal homes, converted castles and palaces, or monasteries are run as *paradores* and offer the most luxurious hotel accommodations.

- *Un hostal* (oon ohs-tahl): This accommodation is a small hotel or inn without a restaurant.

- *Un refugio* (oon rreh-foo-hee-yoh): *Un refugio* is a private retreat or lodge in the country that may be rented for a specified time period and is popular with hunters, hikers, and fisherman.

What a Place! Does It Have ... ?

Before leaving home, you probably should check with your travel agent or the hotel's management to make sure the hotel you've chosen has the amenities you desire. Depending on your requirements, you need to know the words for everything from bathroom to swimming pool. Even with reservations, you'll end up with some surprises—but it never hurts to ask questions when you are making arrangements. See Table 8.1 for a basic list of hotel amenities.

Is (Are) there …?
¿Hay …?
Ahy

Table 8.1   Hotel Facilities

Term	Spanish	Pronunciation
a bar	un bar	oon bahr
a bellman	un portero	oon pohr-teh-roh
a business center	un centro de negocios	oon sehn-troh deh neh-goh-see-yohs
a concierge (caretaker)	un conserje	oon koh-sehr-heh
a doorman	un portero	oon pohr-teh-roh
an elevator	un ascensor	oon ah-sehn-sohr
a fitness center	un gimnasio	oon heem-nah-see-yoh
a gift shop	una tienda de regalos	oo-nah tee-yehn-dah deh rreh-gah-lohs

continues

Table 8.1 (continued)

Term	Spanish	Pronunciation
a laundry and dry cleaning service	una lavandería	oo-nah lah-bahn-deh-ree-yah
maid service	una gobernanta	oo-nah goh-behr-nahn-tah
a restaurant	un restaurante	oon rrehs-tow-rahn-teh
a staircase	una escalera	oo-nah ehs-kah-leh-rah
a swimming pool	una piscina	oo-nah pee-see-nah
valet parking	una atendencia del garaje	oo-nah ah-tehn-dehn-see-yah dehl gah-rah-heh

¡Cuidado!

In Spanish buildings, the ground floor is called *la planta baja* (lah plahn-tah bah-hah), which literally means "the lower floor." The basement is called *el sótano* (ehl soh-tah-noh). Expect to see the abbreviations PB and Sót. for these levels on elevator buttons. The word *piso* (pee-soh) refers to floors above ground level.

Checking In to Your Hotel

When you check in you may want to ask for the following:

I'd like a double (single) room, please.
Quisiera una habitación con dos camas (una sola cama).
kee-see-yeh-rah oo-nah ah-bee-tah-see-yohn
kohn dohs kah-mahs (oo-nah soh-lah kah-mah)

I don't have a reservation.
No tengo reserva.
noh tehn-goh rreh-sehr-bah

May I see the room?
¿Puedo ver la habitación?
poo-weh-doh behr lah ah-bee-tah-see-yohn

What is the room number?
¿Cuál es el número de la habitación?
kwahl ehs ehl noo-meh-roh deh lah ah-bee-tah-
see-yohn

What floor is it on?
¿En qué piso está?
ehn keh pee-soh ehs-tah

Is everything included?
¿Está incluído todo?
ehs-tah een-kloo-ee-doh toh-doh

I (don't) like it.
(No) Me gusta.
(noh) meh goos-tah

Could you put another bed in the room?
¿Podría poner otra cama en la habitación?
poo-dree-yah poh-nehr oh-trah kah-mah ehn lah
ah-bee-tah-see-yohn

How much is the room?
¿Cuánto cuesta la habitación?
kwahn-toh kwehs-tah lah ah-bee-tah-see-yohn

> with breakfast
> *con desayuno*
> kohn deh-sah-yoo-noh

> without meals
> *sin comidas*
> seen koh-mee-dahs

How much extra do we have to pay?
¿Cuánto más tenemos que pagar?
kwahn-toh mahs teh-neh-mohs keh pah-gahr

May I please have the key?
¿Puedo obtener la llave, por favor?
pweh-doh ohb-teh-nehr lah yah-beh pohr fah-bohr

Getting What You Want

Is something missing? Are you dissatisfied with your accommodations? If you need something to make your stay more enjoyable, don't be afraid to speak up. Table 8.2 lists a few items you might want or need.

I would like...	Please send me ...
Quisiera ...	*Haga el favor de mandarme ...*
kee-see-yeh-rah	hah-gah ehl fah-bohr deh mahn-dahr-meh
I need ...	There isn't (aren't) ...
Me falta(n) ...	*No hay ...*
meh fahl-tah(n)	noh ahy

I need …
Necesito …
neh-seh-see-toh

Table 8.2   Wants and Needs

Phrase	Spanish	Pronunciation
air conditioning	aire acondicionado	ahy-reh ah-kohn-dee-syoh-nah-doh
an alarm clock	un despertador	dehs-pehr-tah-dohr
an ashtray	un cenicero	oon seh-nee-seh-roh
a balcony	un balcón	oon bahl-kohn
a bar of soap	una pastilla de jabón	oo-nah pahs-tee-yah deh hah-bohn
a bathroom (private)	un baño (privado)	oon bah-nyoh (pree-bah-doh)
a bellhop	un botones	oon boh-toh-nehs
a blanket	una manta	oo-nah mahn-tah
a chambermaid	una camarera	oo-nah kah-mah-reh-rah
a hair dryer	un secador de pelo	oon seh-kah-dohr deh peh-loh
hangers	unas perchas	oo-nahs pehr-chahs
ice cubes	cubitos de hielo	hoo-bee-tohs deh yeh-loh
a key	una llave	oo-nah yah-beh
mineral water	agua mineral	ah-gwah mee-neh-rahl
on the courtyard	con vista al patio	kohn bees-tah ahl pah-tee-yoh

continues

Table 8.2 (continued)

Phrase	Spanish	Pronunciation
on the garden	con vista al jardín	kohn bees-tah ahl har-deen
on the sea	con vista al mar	kohn bees-tah ahl mahr
a pillow	una almohada	oo-nah ahl-moh-hah-dah
a roll of toilet paper	un rollo de papel higiénico	oon rroh-yoh deh pah-pehl ee-hee-yeh-nee-koh
a room	una habitación	oo-nah ah-bee-tah-see-yohn
a safe (deposit box)	una caja de seguridad	oo-nah kah-hah deh seh-goo-ree-dahd
a shower	una ducha	oo-nah doo-chah
single (double) room	una habitación con una sola cama (con dos camas)	oo-nah ah-bee-tah-see-yohn kohn oo-nah soh-lah kah-mah (kohn dohs kah-mahs)
a telephone (dial-direct)	un teléfono (directo)	oon teh-leh-foh-noh (dee-rehk-toh)
a television (color)	una televisión (en color)	oo-nah teh-leh-bee-see-yohn (ehn koh-lohr)
tissues	pañuelos de papel	pah-nyoo-weh-lohs deh pah-pehl
toilet facilities	un W.C.	oon doh-bleh-beh seh
a towel	una toalla	oo-nah toh-wah-yah
a transformer (an electric adaptor)	un transformador	oon trahns-fohr-mah-dohr

Bathroom Etiquette

In many foreign countries, especially in older establishments, the sink and bathtub (and/or shower) are located in what is called the bathroom—*el baño* (ehl bah-nyoh)—while the toilet and bidet are in the water closet—*el W.C.* (ehl doh-bleh-beh seh). Showers are often of the hand-held type and are not affixed to the wall, which sometimes makes them rather difficult to negotiate. A bidet is a marvelous accessory that can be found in many foreign countries. It allows a person to clean his or her private parts in a very discreet way. The user must face forward, straddle the bidet, and manually turn on controlled jets of hot and cold water. Please use it properly. It is not for feet or dirty laundry.

When There's a Problem

Upon arrival, it is not uncommon to find that your room isn't exactly what you expected. Use the following phrases when you have a problem:

I don't like the room.
No me gusta la habitación.
noh meh goos-tah lah ah-bee-tah-see-yohn

Do you have something …?
¿Hay algo …?
ahy ahl-goh

better	*mejor*	meh-hohr
cheaper	*más barato*	mahs bah-rah-toh
bigger	*más grande*	mahs grahn-deh
quieter	*más privado*	mahs pree-bah-doh
smaller	*más pequeño*	mahs peh-keh-nyoh

The lamp doesn't work.
La lámpara no funciona.
lah lahm-pah-rah noh foonk-see-yoh-nah

Can you fix it as soon as possible?
¿Puede arreglarlo lo más pronto posible?
pweh-deh ah-rreh-glahr-loh loh mahs
prohn-toh poh-see-bleh

Up, Up, and Away

We've all had an elevator experience—either in a hotel or elsewhere—in which we've felt like a large sardine in a small can. When you're pushed to the back or squished to the side, you have to hope that a kind and gentle soul will wiggle a hand free and ask, "*¿Qué piso, por favor?*" You will need the ordinal numbers in Table 8.3 to give a correct answer, such as "*El segundo piso, por favor.*"

Table 8.3 Ordinal Numbers

No.	Spanish	Pronunciation	No.	Spanish	Pronunciation
1st	primero	pree-meh-roh	6th	sexto	sehks-toh
2nd	segundo	seh-goon-doh	7th	séptimo	sehp-tee-moh
3rd	tercero	tehr-seh-roh	8th	octavo	ohk-tah-boh
4th	cuarto	kwahr-toh	9th	noveno	noh-beh-noh
5th	quinto	keen-toh	10th	décimo	deh-see-moh

When using ordinal numbers, keep the following in mind:

- Change the final -*o* of the masculine form to -*a* to make ordinal numbers feminine.

el segundo acto	the second act
la segunda escena	the second scene

- In Spanish, only use ordinal numbers through the tenth. After that, cardinal numbers are used.

la Tercera Avenida	Third Avenue
la página treinta	page 30

¡Cuidado!

When a cardinal number is used as an ordinal number, it is always masculine because the word *número*, which is masculine, is understood.

la página doscientos
page 200

- The words *primero* and *tercero* drop their final -*o* before a masculine, singular noun.

el primer hombre	the first man
la primera mujer	the first woman
el tercer día	the third day
la tercera semana	the third week
BUT	
el siglo tercero	the third century

Chapter 9

It's a Beautiful Morning!

In This Chapter

- The weather
- Days of the week
- Months of the year
- Seasons
- Remembering a date

Whenever you plan a trip, you need to know what weather to anticipate so you can plan and pack properly. Remember that in South American countries below the Equator, the seasons are the opposite of what we experience here. And after you arrive in a country, you'll want to be able to read or listen to the weather forecast (*el pronóstico*, ehl proh-nohs-tee-koh) so you can arrange your sightseeing trips and outings accordingly. The phrases in Table 9.1 will help you with the weather.

Table 9.1 Weather Expressions

Expression	Spanish	Pronunciation
What's the weather?	¿Qué tiempo hace?	keh tee-yehm-poh ah-seh
It's beautiful.	Hace buen tiempo.	ah-seh bwehn tee-yehm-poh
It's hot.	Hace calor.	ah-seh kah-lohr
It's sunny.	Hace sol.	ah-seh sohl
It's nasty (bad).	Hace mal tiempo.	ah-seh mahl tee-yehm-poh
It's cold.	Hace frío.	ah-seh free-yoh
It's cool.	Hace fresco.	ah-seh frehs-koh
It's windy.	Hace viento.	ah-seh bee-yehn-toh
It's lightning.	Hay relámpagos.	ahy rreh-lahm-pah-gohs
It's thundering.	Truena.	troo-weh-nah
It's foggy.	Hay niebla. Hay neblina.	ahy nee-eh-blah ahy neh-blee-nah
It's humid.	Hay humedad.	ahy oo-meh-dahd
It's cloudy.	Hay nubes. Está nublado.	ahy noo-behs ehs-tah noo-blah-doh
It's overcast.	Está cubierto.	ehs-tah koo-bee-yehr-toh
It's raining.	Llueve. Está lloviendo.	yoo-weh-beh ehs-tah yoh-bee-yehn-doh
It's pouring.	Hay lluvias torrenciales.	ahy yoo-bee-yahs toh-rrehn-see-yahl-ehs
It's snowing.	Nieva. Está nevando.	nee-eh-bah ehs-tah neh-bahn-doh

Expression	Spanish	Pronunciation
There'a windstorm.	Hay un vendaval.	ahy oon behn-dah-vahl
There's hail.	Hay granizo.	ahy grah-nee-soh
There are showers.	Hay lluvias.	ahy yoo-bee-ahs

Baby, It's Hot Outside!

Expressing the temperature is different in Spanish-speaking countries. Why? They use the Celsius scale rather than the Fahrenheit scale to which we are accustomed. This means that when the concierge tells you it's 20 degrees (Celsius), it's really a pleasant 68 degrees Fahrenheit. (To convert Centigrade to Fahrenheit, multiply the Centigrade temperature by ⅘ and then add 32.) To ask for the temperature, simply say:

> What's the temperature?
> *¿Cuál es la temperatura?*
> kwahl ehs lah tehm-peh-rah-too-rah

> It's 50 degrees.
> *Hay una temperatura de cincuenta grados.*
> ahy oo-nah tehm-peh-rah-too-rah deh seen-kwehn-tah grah-dos

> It's zero degrees.
> *Hay una temperatura de cero.*
> ahy oo-nah tehm-peh-rah-too-rah deh seh-roh

> It's two degrees below zero.
> *Hay una temperatura de menos dos grados.*
> ahy oo-nah tehm-peh-rah-too-rah deh meh-nohs dohs grah-dos

What Day Is It?

The more preoccupied you are or the busier you get, the more likely you are to forget the day of the week. When traveling, it's very important to keep track of your days so you don't wind up at a tourist attraction you absolutely had to see on the day it is closed. Be careful! Unlike our calendars, Spanish calendars start with Monday. Study the days of the week in Table 9.2 so you don't miss a thing.

In Spanish, only capitalize days of the week when they are at the beginning of a sentence. When used elsewhere, unlike in English, they are written with a lowercase first letter.

> *Sábado es un día.*
> Saturday is a day.
>
> *Voy al supermercado el sábado.*
> I go to the supermarket on Saturday.

Table 9.2   Days of the Week

Day	Spanish	Pronunciation
Monday	lunes	loo-nehs
Tuesday	martes	mahr-tehs
Wednesday	miércoles	mee-yehr-koh-lehs
Thursday	jueves	hoo-weh-behs
Friday	viernes	bee-yehr-nehs
Saturday	sábado	sah-bah-doh
Sunday	domingo	doh-meen-goh

Something Extra

To express "on" when talking about a certain day, the Spanish use the definite article *el.*

Voy al cine el viernes.
I go to the movies on Friday(s).

My Favorite Month

As you glance through glossy vacation brochures, you want to be able to figure out the best time to take your trip. Table 9.3 gives you the names of the months so you don't wind up in the wrong place at the wrong time.

Table 9.3   Months of the Year

Month	Spanish	Pronunciation
January	enero	eh-neh-roh
February	febrero	feh-breh-roh
March	marzo	mahr-soh
April	abril	ah-breel
May	mayo	mah-yoh
June	junio	hoo-nee-yoh
July	julio	hoo-lee-yoh
August	agosto	ah-gohs-toh
September	septiembre	sehp-tee-yehm-breh
October	octubre	ohk-too-breh
November	noviembre	noh-bee-yehm-breh
December	diciembre	dee-see-yehm-breh

Unless used at the beginning of a sentence, the names of all months should be written all lowercase.

> *Enero es un mes.*
> January is a month.
> *Voy a España en enero.*
> I go to Spain in January.

To Every Season Turn, Turn, Turn

Some seasons are better than others for traveling in certain countries. Make sure to plan your trip for when the weather will be great so you don't have to worry about hurricanes, storms, or other adverse conditions. Table 9.4 provides the names of the seasons.

Table 9.4 The Seasons

Season	Spanish	Pronunciation
winter	el invierno	ehl een-bee-yehr-noh
spring	la primavera	lah pree-mah-beh-rah
summer	el verano	ehl beh-rah-noh
autumn, fall	el otoño	ehl oh-toh-nyoh

When's Our Date?

No doubt, when making travel plans and arrangements, you often will have to refer to and ask for dates. Ask the following questions when you need information about the day and the date:

What day is it (today)?
¿Qué día es (hoy)?
keh dee-yah ehs (oy)

What is today's date?
¿A cuántos estamos hoy?
ah kwahn-tohs ehs-tah-mohs oy

What is (today's) the date?
¿Cuál es la fecha (de hoy)?
kwahl ehs lah feh-chah (deh oy)

The Spanish use the preposition *en* + the definite
article for all seasons to express "in." Here's how it's
done:

> *Voy a México en el invierno, en la primavera, en*
> *el verano, y en el otoño.*
> I go to Mexico in the winter, in the spring,
> in the summer, and in the fall.

You need to know how to express the date for
appointments, travel plans, and meetings. In Spanish-
speaking countries, the date is expressed as follows:

> day of week + *el* + (cardinal) number + *de* +
> month + *de* + year
> *Hoy es sábado el nueve de mayo de dos mil tres.*
> *Estamos a sábado el nueve de mayo de dos mil tres.*
> Today is Saturday, May 9, 2003.

Use *primero* to express the first of each month.

> *el primero de mayo*
> May 1

BUT

el veintiuno de mayo
May 21

el dos de mayo
May 2

¡Cuidado!

Notice how the date is written in Spanish:

el 14 de septiembre de 1947 (14.9.47)

September 14, 1947 (9/14/47)

Remember to reverse the month/day sequence used in English.

Do not use hundreds, as we do in English, when giving the year.

mil novecientos noventa y nueve
1999

Use the definite article to express "on" with dates.

Me voy el once de julio.
I'm leaving on July 11.

Chapter 10

Sightseeing

In This Chapter

- Sights for tourists
- How to make suggestions and plans
- How to give your opinion

When you travel to a foreign country, make sure to plan a logical itinerary of interesting sights to see. All the important tourist attractions you want to see for the day should be grouped in the same general vicinity. Running back and forth across a city will waste your precious vacation time. Always have a good game plan!

There's much to do and see in all the Spanish-speaking countries. Decide whether you are in the mood for sightseeing or for relaxing. Do you want to pack your day with activity or do you prefer to proceed at a leisurely pace? The brochures you've picked up at your hotel or at the tourist office will offer many suggestions.

Seeing the Sights

Whether you decide to go it alone or opt to take a tour, the following phrases will come in handy:

> Where is there a tourist office?
> *¿Dónde hay una oficina de turismo?*
> dohn-deh ahy oo-nah oh-fee-see-nah deh too-rees-moh

> What is there to see?
> *¿Qué hay a ver?*
> keh ahy ah behr

> Where can I buy a map (a guide book)?
> *¿Dónde puedo comprar un mapa (una guía)?*
> dohn-deh pweh-doh kohm-prahr oon mah-pah (oo-nah gee-yah)

> At what time does it open (close)?
> *¿A qué hora se abre (se cierra)?*
> ah keh oh-rah seh ah-breh (seh see-yeh-rah)

> What's the admission price?
> *¿Cuánto es la entrada?*
> kwahn-toh ehs lah ehn-trah-dah

> Can children enter for free?
> *¿Pueden entrar gratis los niños?*
> pweh-dehn ehn-trahr grah-tees lohs nee-nyohs

> Until what age?
> *¿Hasta qué edad?*
> ahs-tah keh eh-dahd

> How much do they pay?
> *¿Cuánto pagan?*
> kwahn-toh pah-gahn

Is it all right to take pictures?
¿Se puede sacar fotos?
seh pweh-deh sah-kahr foh-tohs

I need a guide who speaks English.
Necesito un guía que habla inglés.
neh-seh-see-toh oon gee-yah keh ah-blah
een-glehs

How much does he (she) charge?
¿Cuánto cobra?
kwahn-toh koh-brah

May I Suggest ...?

You've always had your heart set on seeing a bull-fight. The fascinating ads, posters, and pictures you've seen have enticed you and have piqued your curiosity. You don't know, however, how the others in your group feel about accompanying you. Go for it! Make the suggestion. There are several easy ways to do this.

Try asking this simple question:

> *¿Por qué no + nosotros* form of the verb?
> Why don't we ...?

> *¿Por qué no vamos al cine?*
> pohr keh noh bah-mohs ahl see-neh
> Why don't we go to the movies?

Try telling a friend what you'd like to do and then ask for his or her feelings about the idea.

Quiero ir al cine. ¿Qué crees (piensas)?
kee-yeh-roh eer ahl see-neh
keh kreh-yehs (pee-yehn-sahs)
I want to go to the movies. What do you think?

Want to say let's? Use *vamos a* + the infinitive of the verb suggesting the activity.

Vamos a ver una corrida de toros.
bah-mohs ah behr oo-nah koh-rree-dah deh
toh-rohs
Let's see a bullfight.

Colloquially Speaking

If you're feeling rather confident with the language at this point, you might want to take a more colloquial approach to expressing yourself. You can use a number of phrases, all of which are followed by the infinitive of the verb. (The familiar *tú* forms are in parentheses.)

Phrase	Pronunciation	Meaning
¿Le (te) parece …?	leh (teh) pah-reh-seh	Do you want …?
¿Le (te) gustaría …?	leh (teh) goos-tah-ree-yah	Would you like …?
¿Tiene(s) ganas de…?	tee-yeh-neh(s) gah-hans deh	Do you feel like …?
¿Quiere(s) …?	kee-yeh-reh(s)	Do you want …?

¿Le (te) gustaría ir al museo?
Would you like to go to the museum?

¿Tiene(s) ganas de ver una corrida de toros?
Do you feel like seeing a bullfight?

Only petulant teenagers give abrupt yes or no answers to questions. Most of the rest of us say "Yes, but ..." or "No, because ..." If you'd like to elaborate on your answer, change the pronoun *le* or *te* from the question to *me* in your answer, as follows:

Sí, me parece ir al museo.
No, no me gustaría ir al museo.

So What Do You Think?

How do you feel about a suggestion made to you? Does the activity appeal to you? If so, you would say:

Me gusta el arte.
meh goos-tah ehl ahr-teh
I like art.

Me encanta la música.
meh ehn-kahn-tah lah moo-see-kah
I adore music.

Soy aficionado(a) a la ópera.
soy ah-fee-see-yoh-nah-doh(dah) ah lah
oh-peh-rah
I'm an opera fan.

When you do something or go somewhere new, different, exotic, or out of the ordinary, you're bound to have an opinion about whether you like it. Is it fun? Are you having a good time? Are you amused? Give your positive opinion by using *es* (ehs, meaning "it is") + an adjective.

Adjective	Spanish	Pronunciation
awesome	bárbaro	bahr-bah-roh
excellent	excelente	ehk-seh-leh-teh
extraordinary	extraordinario	ehs-trah-ohr-dee-nah-ree-yoh
fabulous	fabuloso	fah-boo-loh-soh
fantastic	fantástico	fahn-tahs-tee-koh
fun	divertido	dee-behr-tee-doh
great	regio	rreh-hee-yoh
magnificent	magnífico	mag-nee-fee-koh
marvelous	maravilloso	mah-rah-bee-yoh-soh
out of this world	de película	deh peh-lee-koo-lah
phenomenal	fenomenal	feh-noh-meh-nahl
sensational	sensacional	sehn-sah-see-yoh-nahl
stupendous	estupendo	ehs-too-pehn-doh
terrific	terrífico	teh-rree-fee-koh

Something Extra

When referring to just one thing, use *me gusta* and *me encanta*. When referring to more than one, use *me gustan* and *me encantan*.

Me gusta el museo.
Me gustan los museos.
Me encanta el arte.
Me encantan el arte y la música.

Perhaps you don't like the suggestion presented. Maybe the activity bores you. To express your dislike, you might say:

Phrase	Spanish	Pronunciation
I don't like ...	No me gusta ...	noh meh goos-tah
I hate ...	Odio, Detesto ...	oh-dee-yoh, deh-tehs-toh
I'm not a fan of ...	No soy aficionado(a) de ...	noh soy ah-fee-see-yoh-nah-doh(dah) deh

To be a good sport, you tried the activity anyway. It was just as you thought—not your cup of tea. To give your negative opinion about an activity, you can use *es* (ehs, meaning "it is") + an adjective.

Adjective	Spanish	Pronunciation
boring	aburrido	ah-boo-rree-doh
disagreeable	desagradable	deh-sah-grah-dah-bleh
a disaster	un desastre	oon deh-sahs-treh
horrible	horrible	oh-rree-bleh
a horror	un horror	oon oh-rrohr
loathsome	asqueroso	ahs-keh-roh-soh
ridiculous	ridículo	rree-dee-koo-loh
silly	tonto	tohn-toh
terrible	terrible	teh-rree-bleh
ugly	feo	feh-yoh

The Shopping Experience

In This Chapter

- Stores
- Clothing, colors, sizes, materials, and designs
- Expressing your opinion

Are you particular about what you buy? Is it important to you to pick out the perfect gift or memento? Do you spend time agonizing over the right color, size, material, and design? Or is shopping such a chore that you choose almost anything you feel will be appropriate? Do you like to bargain? How about comparison shopping? No matter what your plan of action, shopping can be made a pleasant and enjoyable experience for everyone.

Do you prefer to browse in chic boutiques? Do you like to bargain in outdoor markets? Or are you attracted by a large, elegant mall (*un centro comercial*, oon sehn-troh koh-mehr-see-yahl)? Table 11.1 points you in the direction of stores (*las tiendas*, lahs tee-yehn-dahs) that might interest you.

Table 11.1   Stores

Store	Store
book store *la librería* lah lee-breh-ree-yah	newsstand *el quiosco de periódicos* ehl kee-yohs-koh deh peh-ree-yoh-dee-kohs
clothing store *la tienda de ropa* lah tee-yehn-dah deh rroh-pah	record store *la tienda de discos* lah tee-yehn-dah deh dees-kohs
department store *el almacén* ehl ahl-mah-sehn	souvenir shop *la tienda de recuerdos* lah tee-yehn-dah deh rreh- kwehr-dohs
florist *la florería* lah floh-reh-ree-yah	tobacco store *la tabaquería* lah tah-bah-keh-ree-yah
jewelry store *la joyería* lah hoh-yeh-ree-yah	toy store *la juguetería* lah hoo-geh-teh-ree-yah
leather goods store *la marroquinería* lah mah-rroh-kee-neh-ree- yah	

If you are buying jewelry, you might want to ask the following questions:

¿Es macizo?
ehs mah-see-soh
Is it solid gold?

¿Es dorado?
ehs doh-rah-doh
Is it gold plated?

¿Es platino?
ehs plah-tee-noh
Is it platinum?

¿Es plata?
ehs plah-tah
Is it silver?

General Questions

Where can I find ...?
¿Dónde se puede encontrar ...?
dohn-deh seh pweh-deh ehn-kohn-trahr

Could you please help me?
¿Podría ayudarme, por favor?
poh-dree-yah ah-yoo-dahr-meh pohr fah-bohr

Would you please show me ...?
¿Pudiera enseñarme ..., por favor?
poo-dee-yeh-rah ehn-seh-nyahr-meh pohr
fah-bohr

Are there any sales?
¿Hay ventas (gangas)?
ahy behn-tahs (gahn-gahs)

Are there any discounts?
¿Hay rebajas (descuentos)
ahy rreh-bah-hahs (dehs-kwehn-tohs)

Do you sell ...?
¿Se vende ...?
seh behn-deh

Where is (are) ...?
¿Dónde está(n) ...?
dohn-deh ehs-tah(n)

Do you have something ...?
¿Tiene algo ...?
tee-yeh-neh ahl-goh

Adjective	Spanish	Pronunciation
else	más	mahs
larger	más grande	mahs grahn-deh

Adjective	Spanish	Pronunciation
smaller	más pequeño	mahs peh-keh-nyoh
longer	más largo	mahs lahr-goh
shorter	más corto	mahs kohr-toh
less expensive	más barato	mahs bah-rah-toh
more expensive	más caro	mahs kah-roh
better	de mejor	deh meh-hor

Does it come in another color?
¿Viene en otro color?
bee-yeh-neh ehn oh-troh koh-lohr

Can I try it on?
¿Puedo probarmelo?
pweh-doh proh-bahr-meh-loh

Can you alter it?
¿Puede arreglarlo?
pweh-deh ah-rreh-glahr-loh

Can I return it?
¿Puedo devolverlo?
pweh-doh deh-bohl-behr-loh

Could you wrap it please?
¿Podría envolverlo, por favor?
poh-dree-yah ehn-bohl-behr-loh pohr fah-bohr

Do you take credit cards?
¿Acepta tarjetas de crédito?
ahk-sehp-tah tahr-heh-tahs deh kreh-dee-toh

Do you take traveler's checks?
¿Acepta cheques de viajero?
ah-sehp-tah cheh-kehs deh bee-yah-heh-roh

Clothing

It's always fun and interesting to buy an item of clothing (*la ropa*, lah roh-pah) in a foreign country. The styles and patterns are really quite unique and often prove to be a topic of conversation. Whether you decide to be daring and buy something native or you crave something at the height of fashion (*a la última moda*, ah lah ool-tee-mah moh-dah), Table 11.2 will help you in your quest.

Table 11.2   Clothing

Clothing	Spanish	Pronunciation
For One and All		
bathing suit	el traje de baño	ehl trah-heh deh bah-nyoh
belt	el cinturón	ehl seen-too-rohn
boots	las botas	lahs boh-tahs
gloves	los guantes	lohs gwahn-tehs
hat	el sombrero	ehl sohm-breh-roh
jacket	la chaqueta	lah chah-keh-tah
jeans	los jeans	lohs jeens
overcoat	el abrigo	ehl ah-bree-goh
pants	los pantalones	lohs pahn-tah-loh-nehs
raincoat	el impermeable	ehl eem-pehr-meh-yah-bleh
robe	la bata	lah bah-tah
sandals	las sandalias	lahs sahn-dah-lee-yahs

continues

Table 11.2 (continued)

Clothing	Spanish	Pronunciation
scarf	la bufanda	lah boo-fahn-dah
shirt	la camisa	lah kah-mee-sah
shoes	los zapatos	lohs sah-pah-tohs
shorts	los pantalones cortos	lohs pahn-tah-loh-nehs kohr-tohs
sneakers	los tenis	lohs teh-nees
socks	los calcetines	lohs kahl-seh-tee-nehs
sweater	el suéter	ehl sweh-tehr
T-shirt	la camiseta, la playera	lah kah-mee-seh-tah, lah plah-yeh-rah
umbrella	el paraguas	ehl pah-rah-gwahs
underwear	la ropa interior	lah rroh-pah een-teh-ree-yohr

For Men Only

coat (sport)	el saco	ehl sah-koh
shorts (under garments)	los calzoncillos	lohs kahl-sohn-see-yohs
suit	el traje	ehl trah-heh
tie	la corbata	lah kohr-bah-tah
undershirt	la camiseta	lah kah-mee-seh-tah

For Women Only

brassiere	el sostén	ehl sohs-tehn
blouse	la blusa	lah bloo-sah
dress	el vestido	ehl behs-tee-doh
negligee	el salto de cama	ehl sahl-toh deh kah-mah

Clothing	Spanish	Pronunciation
panties	los pantaloncillos de mujer	lohs pahn-tah-lohn-see-yohs deh moo-hehr
pantyhose (tights)	las pantimedias	lahs pahn-tee-meh-dee-yahs
pocketbook	la bolsa	lah bohl-sah
skirt	la falda	lah fahl-dah
slip(half) (full)	el faldellín la combinación	ehl fahl-deh-yeen lah kohm-bee-nah-see-yohn
stockings	las medias	lahs meh-dee-yahs
suit	el traje sastre	ehl trah-heh sahs-treh

Of course, you want to make sure you wind up with items that fit. Tell the salesperson the following:

I wear size …	small	medium	large
Llevo el tamaño … yeh-boh ehl tah-mah-nyoh	*pequeño* peh-keh-nyoh	*mediano* meh-dee-yah-noh	*grande* grahn-deh

Colors

Do you see the world in primary colors (*los colores*, lohs koh-loh-rehs)? Or do you tend to go for the more exotic, artistic shades? Table 11.3 will help you learn the basic colors so you can get by.

Table 11.3 Colors

Color	Spanish	Pronunciation
beige	beige	beh-heh
black	negro	neh-groh
blue	azul	ah-sool
brown	marrón, pardo	mah-rrohn, pahr-doh
gray	gris	grees
green	verde	behr-deh
orange	anaranjado	ah-nah-rahn-hah-doh
pink	rosado	rroh-sah-doh
purple	morado	moh-rah-doh
red	rojo	rroh-hoh
white	blanco	blahn-koh
yellow	amarillo	ah-mah-ree-yoh

Add the word *claro* (klah-roh) to describe a color as light. Add the word *oscuro* (oh-skoo-roh) to describe a color as dark.

light green   dark blue
verde claro   *azul oscuro*

Materials

While traveling, you might be tempted to make a clothing purchase. Do you find linen sexy? Do you love the feel of silk? Do you crave the coolness of cotton? Is leather a turn-on? Are you into wrinkle-free? We choose or reject different fabrics for a wide variety of reasons. Table 11.4 will help you pick the materials (*las telas*, lahs teh-lahs) you prefer for your special purchases. Use the word *en* (ehn) in when speaking about materials.

Table 11.4   Materials

Material	Spanish	Pronunciation
cashmere	casimir	kah-see-meer
cotton	algodón	ahl-goh-dohn
denim	tela tejana	teh-lah teh-hah-nah
flannel	franela	frah-neh-lah
lace	encaje	ehn-kah-heh
leather	cuero	kweh-roh
linen	hilo	ee-loh
nylon	nilón	nee-lohn
satin	raso	rrah-soh
silk	seda	seh-dah
suede	gamuza	gah-moo-sah
wool	lana	lah-nah

Designs

Let's say you're on the hunt for a skirt like the ones worn by Spanish *señoritas*. Or maybe you'd like a plaid pair of golf pants because you really want to stand out. Or perhaps you're not even in the mood to shop, but you'd like to compliment someone on the good taste of his striped tie. Table 11.5 provides the words you need to describe patterns or designs (*los diseños*, lohs dee-seh-nyohs).

Table 11.5 Designs

Design	Spanish	Pronunciation
in a solid color	de color liso	deh koh-lohr lee-soh
with stripes	de rayas	deh rrah-yahs
with polka dots	de lunares	deh loo-nah-rehs
in plaid	de cuadros	deh kwah-drohs

Use a demonstrative adjective to express this, that, these, or those. Note that the adjective you choose depends upon the physical proximity of the noun to the subject.

Adjective	Masculine	Femimine
this	este (ehs-teh)	esta (ehs-tah)
these	estos (ehs-tohs)	estas (ehs-tahs)
that (near speaker)	ese (eh-seh)	esa (eh-sah)
those (near speaker)	esos (eh-sohs)	esas (eh-sahs)
that (far from speaker)	aquel (ah-kehl)	aquella (ah-keh-yah)
those (far from speaker)	aquellos (ah-keh-yohs)	aquellas (ah-keh-yahs)

Chapter 12

Food for Thought

In This Chapter

- Buying food
- How to express quantity
- How to order in a restaurant
- How to get the dish you want
- Special diets

Whether you stop by a local bodega or specialty store to grab a bite to tide you over or you make reservations in the fanciest of restaurants, you need to know how to ask for the foods you want and how to refuse those that don't have any appeal. You'll also want to make sure you order the proper quantity. This chapter will help you satisfy all your cravings.

Specialty Shops

Do you like to keep snacks in your hotel room, just in case you get the midnight munchies? Or have you rented a condo or an apartment and prefer to do your own cooking? In any Spanish-speaking country, you can enjoy the culinary delights that can be purchased in the shops listed in Table 12.1.

Table 12.1 Food Shops

grocery (vegetable) store	la abacería lah ah-bah-seh-ree-yah
butcher shop	la carnicería lah kahr-nee-seh-ree-yah
bakery	la panadería lah pah-nah-deh-ree-yah
delicatessen	la salchichonería lah sahl-chee-choh-neh-ree-yah
candy store	la confitería lah kohn-fee-teh-ree-yah
dairy store	la lechería lah leh-cheh-ree-yah
fruit store	la frutería lah froo-teh-ree-yah
pastry shop	la pastelería lah pahs-teh-leh-ree-yah
fish store	la pescadería lah pehs-kah-deh-ree-yah
supermarket	el supermercado ehl soo-pehr-mehr-kah-doh
liquor store	la tienda de licores lah tee-yehn-dah deh lee-koh-rehs

Many stores take their name from the product they sell, as follows:

pan	*panadería*
carne	*carnicería*

pastel	*pastelería*
leche	*lechería*
fruta	*frutería*
pescado	*pescadería*

Food and More Food

Whether you're in a store or at a restaurant, knowing the Spanish names of the foods you like and dislike will put you at a distinct advantage. Use Tables 12.2 through 12.9 to pick and choose at will.

Table 12.2 Vegetables *(Las Legumbres)*

Vegetable	Spanish	Pronunciation
asparagus	los espárragos	lohs ehs-pah-rrah-gohs
beans (green)	las judías	lahs hoo-dee-yahs
beet	la remolacha	lah rreh-moh-lah-chah
broccoli	el brécol	ehl breh-kohl
carrot	la zanahoria	lah sah-nah-hoh-ree-yah
cauliflower	la coliflor	lah koh-lee-flohr
celery	el apio	ehl ah-pee-yoh
chickpeas	los garbanzos	lohs gahr-bahn-sohs
corn	el maíz	ehl mah-yees
cucumber	el pepino	ehl peh-pee-noh
eggplant	la berenjena	lah beh-rehn-heh-nah
lettuce	la lechuga	lah leh-choo-gah
mushroom	el champiñon	ehl chahm-pee-nyohn
onion	la cebolla	lah seh-boh-lyah

continues

Table 12.2 (continued)

Vegetable	Spanish	Pronunciation
peas	los guisantes	lohs gee-sahn-tehs
pepper	el pimiento	ehl pee-mee-yehn-toh
potato	la papa, la patata	lah pah-pah, lah pah-tah-tah
rice	el arroz	ehl ah-rohs
spinach	la espinaca	lah ehs-pee-nah-kah
squash	la cucurbitácea	lah koo-koor-bee-tah-seh-yah
sweet potato	la papa dulce	lah pah-pah dool-seh
tomato	el tomate	ehl toh-mah-teh
zucchini	el calabacín	ehl kah-lah-bah-seen

Table 12.3 Fruits (Las Frutas)

Fruit	Spanish	Pronunciation
apple	la manzana	lah mahn-sah-nah
apricot	el albaricoque	ehl ahl-bah-ree-koh-keh
banana (green)	la banana (el plátano)	lah bah-nah-nah (ehl plah-tah-noh)
blueberry	el mirtilo	ehl meer-tee-loh
cherry	la cereza	lah seh-reh-sah
coconut	el coco	ehl koh-koh
grape	la uva	lah oo-bah
grapefruit	el pomelo	ehl poh-meh-loh
lemon	el limón	ehl lee-mohn
lime	la lima	lah lee-mah
melon	el melón	ehl meh-lohn

Fruit	Spanish	Pronunciation
olive	la aceituna	lah ah-seh-yee-too-nah
orange	la naranja	lah nah-rahn-hah
peach	el melocotín	ehl meh-loh-koh-teen
pear	la pera	lah peh-rah
pineapple	la piña	lah pee-nyah
plum	la ciruela	lah see-roo-weh-lah
prune	la ciruela pasa	lah see-roo-weh-lah pah-sah
raisin	la uva seca	lah oo-bah seh-kah
raspberry	la frambuesa, la mora	lah frahm-bweh-sah, lah moh-rah
strawberry	la fresa	lah freh-sah
watermelon	la sandía	lah sahn-dee-yah

Table 12.4   Meats (Las Carnes)

Meat	Spanish	Pronunciation
beef	la carne de vaca	lah kahr-neh deh bah-kah
chop, cutlet	la chuleta	lah choo-leh-tah
chopped meat	la carne picada	lah kahr-neh pee-kah-dah
filet mignon	el lomo fino	ehl loh-moh fee-noh
ham	el jamón	ehl hah-mohn
hamburger	la hamburguesa	lah ahm-boor-geh-sah
lamb	la carne de cordero	lah kahr-neh deh kohr-deh-roh
liver	el hígado	ehl ee-gah-doh
pork	la carne de cerdo	lah kahr-neh deh sehr-doh

continues

Table 12.4   (continued)

Meat	Spanish	Pronunciation
roast beef	el rosbíf	ehl rrohs-beef
sausage	el chorizo	ehl choh-ree-zoh
steak	el bistec	ehl bees-tehk
stew	el estofado, el guisado	ehl ehs-toh-fah-doh, ehl gee-sah-doh
veal	la carne de ternera	lah kahr-neh deh tehr-neh-rah

Table 12.5   Fowl and Game *(La Carne Ave y de Caza)*

Fowl or Game	Spanish	Pronunciation
chicken	el pollo	ehl poh-yoh
duck	el pato	ehl pah-toh
rabbit	el conejo	ehl koh-neh-hoh
turkey	el pavo	ehl pah-boh

Table 12.6   Fish and Seafood *(El Pescado y Los Mariscos)*

Fish or Seafood	Spanish	Pronunciation
anchovy	la anchoa	la ahn-choh-ah
bass	la merluza	lah mehr-loo-sah
clam	la almeja	lah ahl-meh-hah
codfish	el bacalao	ehl bah-kah-lah-oh
crab	el cangrejo	ehl kahn-greh-hoh

Fish or Seafood	Spanish	Pronunciation
flounder	el lenguado	ehl lehn-gwah-doh
grouper	el mero	ehl meh-roh
lobster	la langosta	lah lahn-gohs-tah
mackerel	la caballa	lah kah-bah-yah
monkfish	el rape	ehl rrah-peh
mussel	el mejillón	lah meh-hee-yohn
oyster	la ostra	lah ohs-trah
red snapper	el pargo colorado	ehl pahr-goh koh-loh-rah-doh
scallops	las conchas de peregrino	lahs kohn-chahs deh peh-reh-gree-noh
shrimp	los camarones, las gambas	lohs kah-mah-roh-nehs, lahs gahm-bahs
sole	el lenguado	ehl lehn-gwah-doh
swordfish	el pez espada	ehl pehs ehs-pah-dah
trout	la trucha	lah troo-chah
tuna	el atún	ehl ah-toon

Table 12.7   Dairy Products (Productos Lácteos)

Dairy Product	Spanish	Pronunciation
butter	la mantequilla	lah mahn-teh-kee-yah
cheese	el queso	ehl keh-soh
cream	la crema	lah kreh-mah
eggs	los huevos	lohs hweh-bohs
yogurt	el yogur	ehl yoh-goohr

Table 12.8 Bakery Items *(Pan y Postres)*

Bread or Dessert	Spanish	Pronunciation
biscuit	el bizcocho	ehl bees-koh-choh
bread	el pan	ehl pahn
cake	el pastel	ehl pahs-tehl
cookie	la galleta	lah gah-yeh-tah
pie	el pastel	ehl pahs-tehl
rice pudding	el arroz con leche	ehl ah-rohs kohn leh-cheh
rolls (sweet)	los panecillos (dulces)	lohs pah-neh-see-yohs (dool-sehs)

Table 12.9 Beverages *(Las Bebidas)*

Drink	Spanish	Pronunciation
beer	la cerveza	lah sehr-beh-sah
champagne	el champán	ehl chahm-pahn
cider	la sidra	lah see-drah
coffee (iced)	el café (helado)	ehl kah-feh (eh-lah-doh)
hot chocolate	el chocolate	ehl choh-koh-lah-teh
juice	el jugo	ehl hoo-goh
lemonade	la limonada	lah lee-moh-nah-dah
milk	la leche	lah leh-cheh
milk shake	el batido de leche	ehl bah-tee-doh deh leh-cheh
mineral water	el agua mineral	ehl ah-gwah mee-neh-rahl
carbonated	con gas	kohn gahs
non-carbonated	sin gas	seen gahs

Drink	Spanish	Pronunciation
soda	la gaseosa	lah gah-seh-yoh-sah
tea (iced)	el té (helado)	ehl teh (eh-lah-doh)
wine	el vino	ehl bee-noh

Getting the Right Amount

In Spanish-speaking countries, the metric system is used when measuring quantities of food. Liquids are measured in liters, and solids are measured in kilograms or fractions thereof. Most of us are used to dealing with ounces, pounds, pints, quarts, and gallons.

Not having been brought up on the metric system, I can understand that you might be a little confused. Sometimes it's just simpler to ask for a box, bag, jar, and so on, and to commit to memory the amounts we're accustomed to—a pound, a quart, and so on. Consult Table 12.10 to easily get the amount you want or need.

Table 12.10   Getting the Amount You Want

Amount	Spanish	Pronunciation
a bag of	un saco de	oon sah-koh deh
a bar of	una tableta de	oo-nah tah-bleh-tah deh
a bottle of	una botella de	oo-nah boh-teh-yah deh
a box of	una caja de	oo-nah kah-hah deh
a can of	una lata de	oo-nah lah-tah deh
a dozen	una docena de	oo-nah doh-seh-nah deh

continues

Table 12.10 (continued)

Amount	Spanish	Pronunciation
a jar of	un pomo de	oon poh-moh deh
a package of	un paquete de	oon pah-keh-teh deh
a piece of	un pedazo de	oon peh-dah-soh deh
a slice of	un trozo de	oon troh-soh deh
a little	un poco de	oon poh-koh deh
a lot	mucho(a)	moo-choh(chah)
enough	bastante, suficiente	bahs-tahn-teh, soo-fee-see-yehn-teh
too much	demasiado	deh-mah-see-yah-doh

It's Mealtime

Breakfast, *el desayuno* (ehl deh-sah-yoo-noh), is generally eaten between 7 A.M. and 9 A.M. in Spanish-speaking countries. It usually is much lighter than its American counterpart, consisting of coffee with milk and bread with butter or jam. *Churros* (fritters made by frying long strips of dough in oil and then sprinkling them with sugar) and chocolate (hot chocolate) are special favorites.

Regional snacks and drinks (*batidas y licuados*) that serve as midmorning snacks are consumed between 10:30 A.M. and noon.

Lunch, *la comida* (lah koh-mee-dah) in Spain and Mexico and *el almuerzo* (ehl ahl-mwehr-soh) in South America and the Caribbean, is eaten between 1:30 P.M. and 3:30 P.M. and is considered the main meal of the day. It includes soup, meat or fish, vegetables, salad, and dessert.

La merienda (lah meh-ree-yehn-dah), a late afternoon snack, is generally served between 5:00 P.M. and 6:00 P.M. It customarily consists of coffee or tea and pastry.

Supper is referred to as *la cena* (lah seh-nah) in Spain and as *la comida* (lah koh-mee-dah) in Spanish America. This meal tends to be light because it is consumed late, sometimes after 9:00 P.M.

To make a reservation in a restaurant be sure to include the necessary information:

I would like to reserve a table …
Quisiera hacer una reserva …
kee-see-yeh-rah ah-sehr oo-nah rreh-sehr-bah

> … for this evening.
> *para esta noche.*
> pah-rah ehs-tah noh-cheh

> … for tomorrow evening.
> *para mañana por la noche.*
> pah-rah mah-nyah-nah pohr lah noh-cheh

> … for Saturday evening.
> *para el sábado por la noche.*
> pah-rah ehl sah-bah-doh pohr lah noh-cheh

> … for two people.
> *para dos personas.*
> pah-rah dohs pehr-soh-nahs

> … for 8:30 P.M.
> *para las ocho y media.*
> pah-rah lahs oh-choh ee meh-dee-yah

> … on the terrace, please (outdoors).
> *en la terraza, por favor.*
> ehn lah teh-rrah-sah pohr fah-bohr

… in the corner.
en el rincón.
ehn ehl rreen-kohn

… near the window.
cerca de la ventana.
sehr-kah deh lah behn-tah-nah

If you do not reserve a table and show up at a restaurant unannounced, *el jefe de comedor* (ehl heh-feh deh koh-meh-dohr), the head waiter, will surely ask the following:

A table for how many?
¿Una mesa para cuántas personas?
oo-nah meh-sah pah-rah kwahn-tahs
pehr-soh-nahs

Make sure to answer his question completely, as follows:

A table for two, please.
Una mesa para dos, por favor.
oo-nah meh-sah pah-rah dohs pohr fah-bohr

At the Table

Let's say you've now been seated. You look around and are delighted with the fine china, the crystal, the linen napkins, and the crisp white table cloth. But wait! Your fork is missing and a glass is chipped. Table 12.11 provides the vocabulary you need when asking the waiter for cutlery or other missing pieces. Remember to say "*Necesito …*" (neh-seh-see-toh) to tell the waiter what you need.

Table 12.11   Tableware *(Servicio de Mesa)*

Tableware	Spanish	Pronunciation
bowl	un tazón	oon tah-sohn
cup	una taza	oo-nah tah-sah
dinner plate	un plato	oon plah-toh
fork	un tenedor	oon teh-neh-dohr
glass	un vaso	oon bah-soh
knife	un cuchillo	oon koo-chee-yoh
menu	un menú	oon meh-noo
napkin	una servilleta	oo-nah sehr-bee-yeh-tah
place setting	un cubierto	oon koo-bee-yehr-toh
saucer	un platillo	oon plah-tee-yoh
soup dish	un sopero	oon soh-peh-roh
soup spoon	una cuchara	oo-nah koo-chah-rah
tablecloth	un mantel	oon mahn-tehl
teaspoon	una cucharita	oo-nah koo-chah-ree-tah
wine glass	una copa	oo-nah koh-pah

The waiter has come to give you a menu and to see whether you'd like a drink before dinner. You can use the following expressions for ordering both your food and drinks:

What is today's specialty?
¿Cuál es el plato del día de hoy?
kwahl ehs ehl plah-toh dehl dee-yah deh oy

What is the house specialty?
¿Cuál es la especialidad de la casa?
kwahl ehs lah ehs-peh-see-yah-lee-dahd deh lah kah-sah

What do you recommend?

¿Qué recomienda Ud.?

keh rreh-koh-mee-yehn-dah oo-stehd

I Need an Explanation

A Spanish menu can be confusing and overwhelming unless you know certain culinary terms. The waiter will probably get lost in his explanation. Table 12.12 gives you the terms you need to know.

Table 12.12 Understanding the Menu

Item	Pronunciation	Meaning
Sauces (Salsas)		
ají de queso	ah-hee deh keh-soh	cheese sauce
adobo	ah-doh-boh	chili sauce made with sesame seeds, nuts, and spices
mole	moh-leh	chili sauce made with sesame seeds, cocoa, and spices
pipían seed	pee-pee-yahn	chili and pumpkin sauce spiced with coriander and served with bread crumbs
salsa cruda	sahl-sah kroo-dah	an uncooked tomato sauce dip
salsa de tomatilla	sahl-sah deh toh-mah-tee-yah	Mexican green tomato sauce
salsa de perejil	sahl-sah deh peh-reh-heel	parsley sauce

Item	Pronunciation	Meaning
verde	behr-deh	green chili and green tomato sauce

Chilies (Chiles)

Item	Pronunciation	Meaning
ancho	ahn-choh	medium hot
chipotle	chee-poh-tehl	hot, smokey flavored
jalapeño	hah-lah-peh-nyoh	hot, meaty flavored
pasilla	pah-see-yah	hot, rich, sweet flavored
pequín	peh-keen	hot
pimiento	pee-mee-yehn-toh	peppery
poblano	poh-blah-noh	medium hot, rich flavored
serrano	seh-rrah-noh	hot

Tortillas (Tortillas)

Item	Pronunciation	Meaning
burrito	boo-ree-toh	flour tortilla with a cheese and meat filling and served with salsa
chalupas pork	chah-loo-pahs	cheese or ground filled tortillas served with a green chili sauce
chilaquiles	chee-lah-kee-lehs	baked layers of tortillas filled alternately with beans, meat, chicken, and cheese
enchiladas	ehn-chee-lah-dahs	soft corn tortillas filled with meat, rice, and cheese and topped with spicy sauce

continues

Table 12.12 (continued)

Item	Pronunciation	Meaning
flautas	flow-tahs	rolled, flute-shaped, deep-fried tortilla sandwiches
quesadillas	keh-sah-dee-yahs	deep-fried tortillas covered with cheese, tomato, and pepper
tacos	tah-kohs	crisp toasted tortillas filled with meat, poultry, or beans and topped with shredded lettuce, cheese, and sauce
tostada	tohs-tah-dah	tortilla chip with different pepper and cheese toppings

Appetizers (Los Aperetivos)

Item	Pronunciation	Meaning
alcachofas	ahl-kah-choh-fahs	artichokes
almejas	ahl-meh-hahs	clams
anguilas	ahn-gee-lahs	smoked eels
ahumadas	ah-oo-mah-dahs	smoked
calamares	kah-lah-mah-rehs	squid
camarones	kah-mah-roh-nehs	shrimp
caracoles	kah-rah-koh-lehs	snails
champiñones	chahm-pee-nyoh-nehs	mushrooms
chorizo	choh-ree-soh	spicy sausage
cigales	see-gah-lehs	crayfish
guacamole	gwah-kah-moh-leh	avocado spread
huevos	hweh-bohs	eggs
melón	meh-lohn	melon
moluscos	moh-loos-kohs	mussels

Item	Pronunciation	Meaning
ostras	ohs-trahs	oysters
sardinas	sahr-dee-nahs	sardines
tostadas	tohs-tah-dahs	tortilla chips
Soups (Las Sopas)		
gazpacho	gahs-pah-choh	puréed uncooked vegetables, served cold
potaje madrileño	poh-tah-heh mah-dree-leh-nyoh	thick, puréed cod, spinach, and chickpeas
sopa de ajo	soh-pah deh ah-hoh	garlic soup
sopa de albóndigas	soh-pah deh ahl-bohn-dee-gahs	meatball soup
sopa de cebolla	soh-pah deh seh-boh-lah	onion soup
sopa de fideos	soh-pah deh fee-deh-yohs	noodle soup
sopa de gambas	soh-pah deh gahm-bahs	shrimp soup
sopa de mariscos	soh-pah deh mah-rees-kohs	seafood soup
sopa de pescado	soh-pah deh pehs-kah-doh	fish soup
sopa de verduras	soh-pah deh behr-doo-rahs	soup made from puréed green vegetables

Proper Preparation

Of course, you want to make sure your meal is cooked just the way you like it. The waiter may ask the following:

How do you want it (them)?
¿Cómo lo (los, la, las) quiere?
koh-moh loh (lohs, lah, lahs) kee-yeh-reh

Table 12.13 will help you express your wants and needs.

Table 12.13 Preparing It Properly

Term	Spanish	Pronunciation
baked	asado	ah-sah-doh
boiled	hervido	ehr-bee-doh
breaded	empanado	ehm-pah-nah-doh
broiled	a la parrilla	ah lah pah-rree-yah
browned	al horno	ahl ohr-noh
chopped	picado	pee-kah-doh
fried	frito	free-toh
grilled	asado a la parrilla	ah-sah-doh ah lah pah-rree-yah
marinated	escabechado	ehs-kah-beh-chah-doh
mashed	puré	poo-reh
poached	escalfado	ehs-kahl-fah-doh
roasted	asado	ah-sah-doh
with sauce	con salsa	kohn sahl-sah
sautéed	salteado	sahl-teh-yah-doh
smoked	ahumado	ah-oo-mah-doh
steamed	al vapor	ahl bah-pohr
stewed	estofado	ehs-toh-fah-doh
very rare	casi crudo	kah-see kroo-doh
rare	poco asado	poh-koh ah-sah-doh
medium rare	un poco rojo pero no crudo	oon poh-koh rroh-hoh peh-roh noh kroo-doh

Term	Spanish	Pronunciation
medium	a término medio	ah tehr-mee-noh meh-dee-yoh
well-done	bien asado (hecho, cocido)	bee-yehn ah-sah-doh (eh-choh, koh-see-doh)
Eggs (Los Huevos)		
fried	fritos	free-tohs
hard-boiled	duros	doo-rohs
poached	escalfados	ehs-kahl-fah-dohs
scrambled	revueltos	rreh-bwehl-tohs
soft-boiled	pasados por agua	pah-sah-dohs poh ah-gwah
omelet	una tortilla	oo-nah tohr-tee-yah
plain omelet	una tortilla francesa	oo-nah tohr-tee-yah frahn-seh-sah
herb omelet	una tortilla con hierbas	oo-nah tohr-tee-yah kohn yehr-bahs

Spice It Up

Different spices are used in Spain and in the Spanish American countries. Depend on menu descriptions or your server to help you determine whether the dish will be to your liking—bland or spicy. Table 12.14 will help you with the spices you might encounter.

Table 12.14   Herbs, Spices, and Condiments (*Hierbas, Especias, y Condimentos*)

Term	Spanish	Pronunciation
basil	la albahaca	lah ahl-bah-ah-kah
butter	la mantequilla	lah mahn-teh-kee-yeh
dill	el eneldo	ehl eh-nehl-doh
garlic	el ajo	ehl ah-hoh
ginger	el jenjibre	ehl hehn-hee-breh
honey	la miel	lah mee-yehl
jam, jelly	la mermelada	lah mehr-meh-lah-dah
ketchup	la salsa de tomate	lah sahl-sah deh toh-mah-teh
lemon	el limón	ehl lee-mohn
mayonnaise	la mayonesa	lah meh-yoh-neh-sah
mustard	la mostaza	lah mohs-tah-sah
oil	el aceite	ehl ah-seh-ee-teh
oregano	el orégano	ehl oh-reh-gah-noh
paprika	el pimentón dulce	ehl pee-mehn-tohn dool-seh
parsley	el perejil	ehl peh-reh-heel
pepper	la pimienta	lah pee-mee-yehn-tah
rosemary	el romero	ehl rroh-meh-roh
saffron	el azafrán	ehl ah-sah-frahn
salt	la sal	lah sahl
sesame	el ajonjolí	ehl ah-hohn-hoh-lee
sugar	el azúcar	ehl ah-soo-kahr
thyme	el tomillo	ehl toh-mee-yoh
vinegar	el vinagre	ehl bee-nah-greh

¡Cuidado!

There is no Spanish word for "some" when the item can't be counted. Use *Quisiera* (kee-see-yeh-rah) + the noun to express what you want, as follows:

Quisisera sal, por favor.
I'd like some salt, please.

Special Requests

If you have certain likes, dislikes, or dietary restrictions that you would like to make known, keep the following phrases handy:

Table 12.15   Dietary Restrictions

Phrase	Spanish	Pronunciation
I am on a diet.	Estoy a régimen.	ehs-toy ah rreh-hee-mehn
I'm a vegetarian.	Soy vegetariano(a).	soy beh-heh-tah-ree-yah-noh(nah)
I can't have …	No puedo tomar …	noh pweh-doh toh-mahr
any dairy products	productos lácteos	proh-dook-tohs lahk-teh-yohs
any alcohol	alcohol	ahl-koh-ohl
any saturated fats	grasas saturadas	grah-sahs sah-too-rah-dahs
any shellfish	mariscos	mah-rees-kohs

continues

Table 12.15 (continued)

Phrase	Spanish	Pronunciation
I'm looking for a dish ...	Estoy buscando un plato ...	ehs-toy boos-kahn-doh oon plah-toh
high in fiber	con mucha fibra	kohn moo-chah fee-brah
low in cholesterol	con poco colesterol	kohn poh-koh koh-lehs-teh-rohl
low in fat	con poca grasa	kohn poh-kah grah-sah
low in sodium	con poca sal	kohn poh-kah sahl
nondairy	non lácteo	nohn lahk-teh-yoh
salt-free	sin sal	seen sahl
sugar-free	sin azúcar	seen ah-soo-kahr
without artificial coloring	sin colorantes artificiales	seen koh-loh-rah-tehs ahr-tee-fee-see-yah-lehs
without preservatives	sin preservativos	seen preh-sehr-bah-tee-bohs

Please Take It Back to the Kitchen

At times, the cooking or the table setting might not be up to your standards. Table 12.16 presents some problems you might encounter.

Table 12.16   Possible Problems

Term	Spanish	Pronunciation
It's cold.	Está frío.	ehs-tah free-yoh
It's too rare.	Está demasiado crudo.	ehs-tah deh-mah-see-yah-doh kroo-doh
It's over-cooked.	Está sobrecocido.	ehs-tah soh-breh-koh-see-doh
It's burned.	Está quemado.	ehs-tah keh-mah-doh
It's too salty.	Está muy salado.	ehs-tah mwee sah-lah-doh
It's too sweet.	Está muy dulce.	ehs-tah mwee dool-seh
It's too spicy.	Está demasiado picante.	ehs-tah deh-mah see-yah-doh pee-kahn-teh
It's bitter (sour).	Está agrio (cortado).	ehs-tah ah-gree-yoh (kohr-tah-doh)
It's dirty.	Está sucio.	ehs-tah soo-see-yoh

Fancy Endings

When it's time for dessert, choose from among the delightful specialties in Table 12.17.

Table 12.17   Daring Desserts

Dessert	In Spanish	Pronunciation
caramel custard	el flan	ehl flahn
cookies	las galletas	lahs gah-yeh-tahs
ice cream	el helado	ehl eh-lah-doh

continues

Table 12.17   (continued)

Dessert	In Spanish	Pronunciation
pie	el pastel	ehl pahs-tehl
sponge cake	el bizcocho	ehl bees-koh-choh
tart	la tarta	lah tahr-tah
yogurt	el yogur	ehl yoh-goor

Table 12.18   Ice Cream

cone	un barquillo	oon bahr-kee-yoh
cup	una copa	oo-nah koh-pah
chocolate	de chocolate	deh choh-koh-lah-teh
vanilla	de vainilla	deh bah-ee-nee-yah
strawberry	de fresa	deh freh-sah
pistachio	de pistacho	deh pees-tah-choh

Table 12.19   Wine

red wine	el vino tinto	ehl bee-noh teen-toh
rosé wine	el vino rosado	ehl bee-noh rroh-sah-doh
white wine	el vino blanco	ehl bee-noh blahn-koh
dry wine	el vino seco	ehl bee-noh seh-koh
sweet wine	el vino dulce	ehl bee-noh dool-seh
sparkling wine	el vino espumoso	ehl bee-noh ehs-poo-moh-soh
champagne	el champán	ehl chahm-pahn

Chapter 13

How to Be a Social Butterfly

In This Chapter

- Amusements and diversions
- Invitations: extending, accepting, and refusing

Are you heading off to the sea to engage in water sports, up to the mountains for skiing or hiking, onto the links for a round of golf, or onto the courts for a brisk tennis match? Are you a film buff or a theatergoer? Do you enjoy a lively opera or an elegant ballet? Perhaps the game's the thing and you'll spend some time with a one-armed bandit in a luxurious casino. With the help of this chapter, you'll be able to do it all—as well as being a guest or doing the inviting.

I Live for Sports

Whether you like to relax as a beach bum, spend your days gazing out at the azure ocean, or feel compelled to engage in every fast-paced sport you can, you need certain words and terms to make your preferences known. Table 13.1 provides a list of sports and outdoor activities. The verbs *hacer** and *jugar* + *a* + definite article** (*el, la, los, las*) are often used to show participation in a sport. Any verb indicated in parentheses is used in place of *jugar* or *hacer*.

I (don't) like …	I (don't) like …
(one sport)	(more than one sport)
(No) Me gusta …	*(No) Me gustan* …
(noh) meh goos-tah …	(noh) meh goos-tahn …

I want to play …
Quiero jugar + *a* + definite article …
kee-yeh-roh hoo-gahr ah

or

Quiero hacer …
kee-yeh-roh ah-sehr

The verb *querer* is irregular and can be followed by the infinitive of a verb:

yo	quiero	kee-yeh-roh
tú	quieres	kee-yeh-rehs
él, ella, Ud.	quiere	kee-yeh-reh
nosotros	queremos	keh-reh-mohs
vosotros	queréis	keh-reh-ees
ellos, ellas, Uds.	quieren	kee-yeh-rehn

We want to play golf.
Nosotros queremos jugar al golf.
nohs-oh-trohs keh-reh-mohs hoo-gahr ahl gohlf

Table 13.1   Sports

Sport	Spanish	Pronunciation
aerobics	los aeróbicos*	lohs ah-yeh-roh-bee-kohs
baseball	el beísbol**	ehl beh-ees-bohl
basketball	el baloncesto**, el básquetbol**	ehl bah-lohn-sehs-toh, ehl bahs-keht-bohl
bicycling	el ciclismo* (montar a bicicleta)	ehl see-klees-moh (mohn-tahr ah bee-see-kleh-tah)
body-building	el culturismo*	ehl kool-too-rees-moh
fishing	la pesca (ir de pesca)	lah pehs-kah (eer deh pehs-kah)
golf	el golf**	ehl gohlf
horseback riding	la equitación*	lah eh-kee-tah-see-yohn
jogging	el footing* (trotar)	ehl foo-teeng (troh-tahr)
sailing	la navegación* (navegar)	lah nah-beh-gah-see-yohn (nah-beh-gahr)
scuba (skin) diving	el buceo (bucear)	ehl boo-seh-yoh (boo-seh-ahr)
soccer	el fútbol**	ehl foot-bohl
surfing	el surf* (surfear)	ehl soorf (soor-feh-yahr)
swimming	la natación* (nadar)	lah nah-tah-see-yohn (nah-dahr)
tennis	el tenis**	ehl teh-nees
volleyball	el volíbol**	ehl boh-lee-bohl
water-skiing	el esquí acuático*	ehl ehs-kee ah-kwah-tee-koh

The verbs *jugar** and *hacer*** are irregular:

Jugar (hoo-gahr)

yo juego (hweh-goh)	nosotros jugamos (hoo-gah-mohs)
tú juegas (hweh-gahs)	vosotros jugáis (hoo-gah-ees)
él, ella, Ud. juega (hweh-gah)	ellos, ellas, Uds. juegan (hweh-gahn)

Hacer (ah-sehr)

yo hago (ah-goh)	nosotros hacemos (ah-seh-mohs)
tú haces (ah-sehs)	vosotros hacéis (ah-seh-ees)
él, ella, Ud. hace (ah-seh)	ellos, ellas, Uds. hacen (ah-sehn)

Sports Equipment

You went on vacation but didn't trust the airlines with your golf clubs and tennis rackets. Or you thought you wouldn't want to play and now you've changed your mind. You can still enjoy your favorite sport if you borrow or rent equipment. Use these phrases when you find yourself in a similar predicament.

> I need …
> *Me falta(n)* …   *Necesito* …
> fahl-tah(n)   neh-seh-see-toh
>
> Could you lend (rent) me …?
> *Podría Ud. prestarme (alquilarme)* …?
> poh-dree-yah oo-stehd prehs-tahr-meh
> (ahl-kee-lahr-meh)

Table 13.2   Sports Equipment *(El Equipo Deportivo)*

Equipment	Spanish	Pronunciation
ball (football, soccer)	la bola	lah boh-lah
ball (baseball, jai alai, tennis)	la pelota	lah peh-loh-tah
ball (basketball)	el balón	ehl bah-lohn
bat	el bate	ehl bah-teh
bicycle	la bicicleta	lah bee-see-kleh-tah
boat	el barco	ehl bahr-koh
canoe	la canoa	lah kah-noh-wah
diving suit	la escafandra	lah ehs-kah-fahn-drah
fishing rod	la caña de pesca	lah kah-nyah deh pehs-kah
golf clubs	los palos de golf	lohs pah-lohs deh gohlf
net	la red	lah rrehd
racquet	la raqueta	lah rrah-keh-tah
skates	los patines	lohs pah-tee-nehs
skis	los esquis	lohs ehs-kees
surfboard	el acuaplano	ehl ah-kwah-plah-noh

Other Amusements

Perhaps sports aren't part of your agenda. There are plenty of other activities you can pursue to have a good time. The phrases in Table 13.3 will give you the tools to make many other intriguing suggestions. Should you delight in going to the opera, the ballet, the theater, or a concert, don't forget to bring along *los gemelos*, binoculars.

Table 13.3 Places to Go

El Lugar (ehl loo-gahr)	Pronunciation	The Place
ir a la opera	eer a lah oh-peh-rah	go to the opera
ir a la playa	eer ah lah plah-yah	go to the pool
ir a una discoteca	eer ah oo-nah dees-koh-teh-kah	go to a disco
ir a un ballet	eer ah oon bah-leht	go to a ballet
ir a un casino	eer ah oon kah-see-noh	go to a casino
ir al centro comercial	eer al sehn-troh koh-mehr-see-yahl	go to the mall
ir al cine	eer al see-neh	go to the movies
ir a un concierto	eer ah oon kohn-see-yehr-toh	go to a concert
ir al teatro	eer al teh-yah-troh	go to the theater
quedarse en su habitación, casa	keh-dahr-seh ehn soo ah-bee-tah-see-yohn, kah-sah	stay in one's room, home

At the Movies and on Television

Do you crave some quiet relaxation? Is the weather bad? Do you feel like getting away from everyone and everything? There's always a movie or the television. It seems that cable has invaded the planet and can accommodate anyone who needs a few carefree hours. If you want to be entertained, consult Table 13.4 for the possibilities.

What kind of film are they showing?
¿Qué tipo de película están dando?
keh tee-poh deh peh-lee-koo-lah ehs-tahn dahn-doh

What's on television?
¿Qué hay en la televisión?
keh ahy ehn lah teh-leh-bee-see-yohn

Table 13.4   Movies and Television Programs

Program Type	Spanish	Pronunciation
adventure film	una película de aventura	oo-nah peh-lee-koo-lah deh ah-behn-too-rah
cartoons	los dibujos animados	lohs dee-boo-hohs ah-nee-mah-dohs
comedy	una comedia	oo-nah koh-meh-dee-yah
game show	un juego	oon hweh-goh
horror movie	una película de horror	oo-nah peh-lee-koo-lah deh oh-rrohr
love story	una película de amor	oo-nah peh-lee-koo-lah deh ah-mohr
mystery	un misterio	oon mees-teh-ree-yoh
news	las noticias	lahs noh-tee-see-yahs
police story	una película policiaca	oo-nah peh-lee-koo-lah poh-lee-see-yah-kah
science-fiction film	una película deciencia ficción	oo-nah peh-lee-koo-lah deh see-yehn-see-yah feek-see-yohn
soap opera	una tele-novela	oo-nah teh-leh-noh-beh-lah
spy movie	una película de espía	oo-nah peh-lee-koo-lah deh ehs-pee-yah
talk show	un programa de entrevistas	oon proh-grah-mah deh ehn-treh-bees-tahs
weather	el parte meteoro-lógico, el pronóstico	ehl pahr-teh meh-teh-yoh-roh-loh-hee-koh, ehl proh-nohs-tee-koh

Refer to the following explanations when you choose a movie or theater:

Forbidden for those under 18 unless accompanied by an adult.
Prohibida para menores de 18 años a menos de que esté acompañado por un adulto.

You must be older than 13.
Mayores de 13 años.

Original version, subtitled.
Versión original.

Dubbed in Spanish.
Versión doblada al español.

Reduced rate.
Tarifa reducida.

So What Did You Think?

If you enjoy the program, you might say:

Phrase	Spanish	Pronunciation
I love it!	¡Me encanta!	meh ehn-kahn-tah
It's a good movie.	Es una buena película.	ehs oo-nah bweh-nah peh-lee-koo-lah
It's amusing!	¡Es divertida!	ehs dee-behr-tee-dah
It's great!	¡Es fantástica!	ehs fahn-tahs-tee-kah
It's moving!	¡Me toca!	meh toh-kah
It's original!	¡Es original!	ehs oh-ree-hee-nahl

If the show leaves something to be desired, try the following phrases:

Phrase	Spanish	Pronunciation
I hate it!	¡La odio!	lah oh-dee-yoh
It's a bad movie!	¡Es una mala película!	ehs oo-nah mah-lah peh-lee-koo-lah
It's a loser!	¡Es un desastre!	ehs oon deh-sahs-treh
It's garbage!	¡Es basura!	ehs bah-soo-rah
It's the same old thing!	¡Siempre es lo mismo!	see-yehm-preh ehs loh mees-moh
It's too violent!	¡Es demasiado violenta!	ehs deh-mah-see-yah-doh bee-yoh-lehn-tah

Invitations

It isn't much fun to play alone. Why not ask someone to join you? To extend an invitation, you can ask the following:

> Do you want to join me (us)?
> *¿Quiere (Quieres) acompañarme (acompañarnos)?*
> kee-yeh-reh (kee-yeh-rehs) ah-kohm-pah-nyahr-meh (ah-kohm-pah-nyahr-nohs)

Whether you've been invited to participate in a sport or an outing, to visit a museum, or just to stay at someone's home, the following phrases will allow you to graciously accept, to cordially refuse, or to show your indifference:

Phrase	Spanish	Pronunciation
	Accepting	
Gladly.	Con placer.	kohn plah-sehr
Great!	¡Magnífico!	mahg-nee-fee-koh
If you want to.	Si tú quieres. (Ud. quiere.)	see too kee-yeh-rehs (oo-stehd kee-yeh-reh)
Okay. (I agree.)	De acuerdo.	deh ah-kwehr-doh
Of course.	Por supuesto.	pohr soo-pwehs-toh
That's a good idea.	Es una buena idea.	ehs oo-nah bweh-nah ee-deh-yah
Why not?	¿Por qué no?	pohr keh noh
With pleasure.	Con mucho gusto.	kohn moo-choh goos-toh
	Refusing	
I'm busy.	Estoy ocupado.	ehs-toy oh-koo-pah-doh
I'm sorry.	Lo siento.	loh see-yehn-toh
I'm tired.	Estoy cansado.	ehs-toy kahn-sah-doh
I can't.	No puedo.	noh pweh-doh
I don't feel like it.	No tengo ganas.	noh tehn-goh gah-nahs
I don't want to.	No quiero.	noh kee-yeh-roh
Not again!	¿Otra vez?	oh-trah behs
	Showing Indifference	
I don't have any preference.	No tengo preferencia.	noh tehn-goh preh-feh-rehn-see-yah
I don't know.	Yo no sé.	yoh noh seh
It depends.	Depende.	deh-peh-deh
Perhaps. Maybe.	Tal vez.	tahl behs
Whatever you want.	Lo que Ud. prefiera (tú prefieras).	loh keh oo-stehd preh-fee-yeh-rah (too preh-fee-yeh-rahs)

Chapter 14

Personal Services

In This Chapter

- At the hairdresser's
- At the dry cleaner's
- At the Laundromat
- At the shoemaker's
- At the optician's
- At the jeweler's
- At the camera shop
- Other services

You've been traveling and having a wonderful time. All of a sudden you have a problem that just can't wait—your roots have surfaced in record time, you spilled tomato sauce on your new white silk shirt, you dropped your contact lens down the drain, you lost a heel on your shoe, or your four-year-old has dropped your camera in the bathtub. You're not home, and you're hesitant about what to do. Don't worry. You just have to know what to say to get the job done. Ask for *las páginas amarillas* (lahs pah-hee-nahs ah-mah-ree-yahs, the Yellow Pages), read the ads, and then explain your problem.

What a Bad Hair Day!

In the past, men went to a *barbería* (bahr-beh-ree-yah, a barber's) while women went to a *salón de belleza* (sah-lohn deh beh-yeh-sah, a beauty parlor). Today, these establishments have become more or less unisex, with men and women demanding more or less the same services. To get what you want simply ask:

Could you give me ...   I would like ...
Podría darme ...   *Quisiera* ...
poh-dree-yah dahr-meh   kee-see-yeh-rah

Today's salons provide the services listed in Table 14.1.

Table 14.1   Hair and Salon Care

Term	Spanish	Pronunciation
a haircut	un corte de pelo	oon kohr-teh deh peh-loh
a manicure	una manicura	oo-nah mah-nee-koo-rah
a pedicure	una pedicura	oo-nah peh-dee-koo-rah
a permanent	una permanente	oo-nah pehr-mah-nehn-teh
a rinse	un aclarado colorante	oon ah-klah-rah-doh koh-loh-rahn-teh
a set	un marcado	oon mahr-kah-doh
a shampoo	un champú	oon chahm-poo
a trim	un recorte	oon rreh-kohr-teh
a waxing	una depilación	oo-nah deh-pee-lah-see-yohn
highlights	reflejos	rreh-fleh-hohs
layers	un corte en capas	oon kohr-teh ehn kah-pahs

Do you need other services? Table 14.2 provides the phrases you need to get them. Use the following phrases to preface your request:

> Could you please …
> *Podría Ud. … por favor*
> poh-dree-yah oo-stehd … pohr fah-bohr

Table 14.2   Other Services

Service	Spanish	Pronunciation
blow dry my hair	secarme el pelo	seh-kahr-meh ehl peh-loh
curl my hair	rizarme el pelo	rree-sahr-meh ehl peh-loh
shave	afeitarme	ah-feh-ee-tahr-meh
my beard	la barba	lah bahr-bah
my mustache	el bigote	ehl bee-goh-teh
my head	la cabeza	lah kah-beh-sah
straighten my hair	estirarme el pelo	ehs-tee-rahr-meh ehl peh-loh
trim my bangs	recortarme el flequillo	rreh-kohr-tahr-meh ehl fleh-kee-yoh
trim	recortarme	rreh-kohr-tahr-meh
my beard	la barba	lah bahr-bah
my mustache	el bigote	ehl bee-goh-teh
my sideburns	las patillas	lahs pah-tee-yahs

Getting What You Want

It's hard enough getting the haircut and style you want when there is no language barrier—imagine the disasters that could befall your poor head in a foreign country! The following phrases will help make your styling and coloring preferences clear to your *peinador* (peh-ee-nah-dor, hairstylist).

> I prefer my hair ...
> *Prefiero mi pelo ...*
> preh-fee-yeh-roh mee peh-loh

> I'd like a ... style.
> *Quisiera un peinado ...*
> kee-see-yeh-rah oon peh-ee-nah-doh

Style	Spanish	Pronunciation
long	largo	lahr-goh
medium	mediano	meh-dee-yah-noh
short	corto	kohr-toh
wavy	ondulado	ohn-doo-lah-doh
curly	rizado	rree-sah-doh
straight	lacio (liso)	lah-see-yoh (lee-soh)

If you don't want certain products on your hair, don't be afraid to tell the hairdresser.

> Don't put on any ... please
> *No me ponga ... por favor*
> noh meh pohn-gah ... pohr fah-bohr

Product	Spanish	Pronunciation
conditioner	suavisante	swah-bee-sahn-teh
gel	gomina, gelatina	goh-mee-nah, geh-lah-tee-nah
hair spray	laca	lah-kah
lotion	loción	loh-see-yohn
mousse	espuma	ehs-poo-mah
shampoo	champú	chahm-poo

Don't forget to ask about tipping:

Is the tip included?
¿Está incluida la propina?
ehs-tah een-kloo-wee-dah lah proh-pee-nah

Problems in General

The following phrases will come in handy when you are seeking certain services or are trying to have something repaired. Use them at the dry cleaner, the shoemaker, the optician, the jeweler, or the camera store.

At what time do you open (close)?
¿A qué hora abre (cierra) Ud.?
ah keh oh-rah ah-breh (see-yeh-reh) oo-sted

What days are you open (closed)?
¿Qué días está Ud. abierto (cerrado)?
keh dee-yahs ehs-tah oo-stehd ah-bee-yehr-toh
(seh-rah-doh)?

Can you fix it (them) today?
¿Puede Ud. arreglarmelo (la, los, las) hoy?
pweh-deh oo-stehd ah-rreh-glahr-meh-loh
(lah, lohs, lahs) oy

Can you fix it (them) temporarily (while I wait)?
*¿Puede Ud. arreglarmelo (la, los, las) temporalmente
(mientras yo espero)?*
pweh-deh oo-stehd ah-rreh-glahr-meh-loh (lah,
lohs, lahs) tehm-poh-rahl-mehn-teh (mee-yehn-
trahs yoh ehs-peh-roh)

How long do I have to wait?
¿Cuánto tiempo tengo que esperar?
kwahn-toh tee-yehm-poh tehn-goh keh
ehs-peh-rahr

How much do I owe you?
¿Cuánto le debo?
kwahn-toh leh deh-boh

Do you accept credit cards (traveler's checks)?
¿Acepta tarjetas de crédito (cheques de viajero)?
ah-sehp-tah tahr-heh-tahs deh kreh-dee-toh
(cheh-kehs deh bee-yah-heh-roh)

May I have a receipt?
¿Me puede dar un recibo?
meh pweh-deh dahr oon rreh-see-boh

At the Dry Cleaner's

You've unpacked. Your white shirt looks like you
slept in it, and your beige pants have an ugly stain
you hadn't noticed before. Don't fret. Your stains,
spots, tears, and wrinkles can be taken care of if you
know how to explain your problem and how to ask
for the necessary service.

I have a problem.	There is (are) …
Tengo un problema.	*Hay …*
tehn-goh oon proh-bleh-mah	ahy

Phrase	Spanish	Pronunciation
a hole	un hueco	oon weh-koh
a missing button	un botón perdido	oon boh-tohn pehr-dee-doh
missing buttons	botones perdidos	boh-toh-nehs pehr-dee-dohs
a spot, a stain	una mancha	oo-nah mahn-chah

Now that you've explained the problem, state what you'd like done about it:

Can you (dry) clean this (these) ... for me?
¿Puede Ud. lavarme este (esta, estos, estas) ... (en seco)?
pweh-deh oo-stehd lah-bahr-meh ehs-teh
(ehs-tah, ehs-tohs, ehs-tahs) ... (ehn seh-koh)

Can you please mend this (these) ... for me?
¿Puede Ud. remendarme este (esta, estos, estas) ...?
pweh-deh oo-stehd rreh-mehn-dahr-meh
ehs-teh (ehs-tah, ehs-tohs, ehs-tahs)

Can you please press (starch) this (these) ... for me?
¿Puede Ud. plancharme (almidonarme) este (esta, estos, estas) ...?
pweh-deh oo-stehd plahn-chahr-meh (ahl-mee-doh-nahr-meh) ehs-teh (ehs-tah, ehs-tohs, ehs-tahs)

I need it (them) ...
Lo (la, los, las) necesito ...
loh (lah, lohs, lahs) neh-seh-see-toh ...

today.	tomorrow.
hoy.	*mañana.*
oy	mah-nyah-nah

this afternoon.	the day after tomorrow.
esta tarde.	*pasado de mañana.*
ehs-tah tahr-deh	pah-sah-doh deh mah-nyah-nah
tonight.	next week.
esta noche.	*la semana próxima.*
ehs-tah noh-cheh	lah seh-mah-nah prohk-see-mah

 Something Extra

If you'd like a service performed for yourself or someone else, use the appropriate indirect object: *me* (for me), *te* (for you), *le* (for him or her), *nos* (for us), *os* (for you), *les* (for them).

Can you please mend this pair of pants for him (her)?
¿Puede Ud. tejerle este pantalón?

At the Laundromat

If your laundry has piled up and you don't mind doing it yourself, you might try to seek out a Laundromat. Use the following phrases to get the information you need:

I'd like to wash my clothes.
Quiero limpiarme la ropa.
kee-yeh-roh leem-pee-yahr-meh lah rroh-pah

I'd like to have my clothes washed.
Quiero que me laven la ropa.
kee-yeh-roh keh meh lah-behn lah rroh-pah

If you want to do the job yourself, the following phrases might serve you well:

Is there a free washing machine (dryer)?
¿Hay una máquina de lavar (secadora) libre?
ahy oo-nah mah-kee-nah deh lah-bahr
(seh-kah-doh-rah) lee-breh

Where can I can buy soap powder?
¿Dónde puedo comprar jabón en polvo?
dohn-deh pweh-doh kohm-prahr hah-bohn ehn
pohl-boh

I need bleach.
Necesito lejía.
neh-seh-see-toh leh-hee-yah

At the Shoemaker's

Let's say you've walked so much you've worn down the soles of your shoes. Perhaps you've broken a shoelace on your dress shoes or you just want a shine. The following phrases will help you describe your problem:

Can you repair ... for me?
¿Puede Ud. remendarme ...?
pweh-deh oo-stehd rreh-mehn-dahr-meh

these shoes	this heel
estos zapatos	*este tacón*
ehs-tohs sah-pah-tohs	ehs-teh tah-kohn

these boots	this sole
estas botas	*esta suela*
ehs-tahs boh-tahs	ehs-tah sweh-lah

Do you sell shoe laces?
¿Vende Ud. cordones de zapato?
behn-deh oo-stehd kohr-doh-nehs deh
sah-pah-toh

I'd like a shoe shine.
Quiero una limpieza de zapatos.
kee-yeh-roh oo-nah leem-pee-yeh-sah deh
sah-pah-tohs

When can I have them?
¿Cuándo los tendrá?
kwahn-doh lohs tehn-drah

I need them by Tuesday (without fail).
Los necesito para el martes (sin falta).
lohs neh-seh-see-toh pah-rah ehl mahr-tehs
(seen fahl-tah)

At the Optician's

What could be more annoying than losing or tearing
a contact lens or breaking or losing a pair of glasses
while away from home? For people who depend on
these optical necessities, the following phrases could
one day prove useful:

Can you repair these glasses for me?
¿Puede Ud. arreglarme estos lentes (estas gafas)?
pweh-deh oo-stehd ah-rreh-glahr-meh ehs-tohs
lehn-tehs (ehs-tahs gah-fahs)

Can you tighten the screws?
¿Puede apretar los tornillitos?
pweh-deh ah-preh-tahr lohs tohr-nee-yee-tohs

The lens (the frame) is broken.
El lente (la montura) está roto(a).
ehl leh-teh (lah mohn-too-rah) ehs-tah
rroh-toh(tah)

I need the glasses as soon as possible.
Necesito las gafas inmediatamente.
neh-seh-see-toh lahs gah-fahs
een-meh-dee-yah-tah-mehn-teh

Can you fix them quickly?
¿Puede repararlas rápidamente?
pweh-deh rreh-pah-rahr-lahs rrah-pee-dah-
mehn-teh

Can you replace this contact lens?
¿Puede Ud. darme otra lentilla (otro lente) de contacto?
pweh-deh oo-stehd dahr-meh oh-trah lehn-tee-
yah (oh-troh lehn-teh) deh kohn-tahk-toh

Do you sell sunglasses?
¿Vende Ud. lentes (gafas) de sol?
behn-deh oo-stehd lehn-tehs (gah-fahs) deh sohl

At the Jeweler's

If your watch has stopped or isn't working as it
should, you might find it necessary to have it
repaired before returning home.

Can you repair this watch?
¿Puede Ud. arreglarme este reloj?
pweh-deh oo-stehd ah-rreh-glahr-meh ehs-teh
rreh-loh?

My watch doesn't work.
Mi reloj no funciona.
mee rreh-loh noh foonk-see-yoh-nah

My watch has stopped.
Mi reloj está parado.
mee rreh-loh ehs-tah pah-rah-doh

My watch is fast (slow).
Mi reloj se adelanta (se atrasa).
mee rreh-loh seh ah-deh-lahn-tah (seh ah-trah-sah)

When will it be ready?
¿Cuándo estará listo?
kwahn-doh ehs-tah-rah lees-toh

Do you sell bands (batteries)?
¿Vende Ud. pulsos (baterías)?
behn-deh oo-stehd pool-sohs (bah-teh-ree-yahs)

At the Camera Shop

For many people, a vacation is not a vacation unless they capture it on film. If you need to visit a camera shop or a film store in a Spanish-speaking country, the following words and phrases will come in handy:

Term	Spanish	Pronunciation
a camera	una cámara	oo-nah kah-mah-rah
film	una película	oo-nah peh-lee-koo-lah
a video camera	una videocámara	oo-nah bee-deh-yoh-kah-mah-rah

If you have special needs, you might ask:

> Can you fix this camera?
> *Puede arreglar esta cámara?*
> pweh-deh ah-rreh-glahr ehs-tah kah-mah-rah

> I need a new battery.
> *Necesito una nueva pila.*
> neh-seh-see-toh oo-nah nweh-bah pee-lah

> How much will the repair cost?
> *¿Cuánto costará el arreglo?*
> kwahn-toh kohs-tah-rah ehl ah-rreh-gloh

> I need it as soon as possible.
> *Lo (la) necesito lo más pronto posible.*
> loh (lah) neh-seh-see-toh loh mahs prohn-toh
> poh-see-bleh

> I would like to have this film developed.
> *Quiero que me revele este carrete (rollo).*
> kee-yeh-roh keh meh rreh-beh-leh ehs-teh
> kah-rreh-teh (rroh-yoh)

Other Services

You also might need special services from time to time. You might, for example, need to find your consulate to report a lost passport. Or perhaps your handbag has been stolen and you'd like to file a police report. You might even want a translator to make sure you don't get into deeper trouble. The following phrases should help:

Where is …?
¿Dónde está …?
dohn-deh ehs-tah

> the police station?
> *la comisaria de policia?*
> lah koh-mee-sah-ree-yah deh poh-lee-see-yah

> the American consulate?
> *el consulado americano?*
> ehl kohn-soo-lah-doh ah-meh-ree-kah-noh

> the American embassy?
> *la embajada americana?*
> lah ehm-bah-hah-dah ah-meh-ree-kah-nah

I lost …
Yo perdí …
yoh pehr-dee

> my passport.   my wallet.
> *mi pasaporte.*   *mi cartera.*
> mee pah-sah-pohr-teh   mee kahr-teh-rah

Help me, please.
Ayúdeme, por favor.
ah-yoo-deh-meh pohr fah-bohr

I need an interpreter.
Necesito un intérprete.
neh-seh-see-toh oon een-tehr-preh-teh

Does anyone here speak English?
¿Hay alguien aquí que hable inglés?
ahy ahl-gee-yehn ah-kee keh ah-bleh een-glehs

Chapter 15

Is There a Doctor on Call?

In This Chapter

- All about your body
- Signs and symptoms
- Illnesses
- Saying how long you've felt this way

Falling ill when you're away from home is hard enough. The situation becomes even tougher if you can't communicate what's wrong. In this chapter, you will learn how to explain your ailments and how long you've been experiencing the symptoms.

Where Does It Hurt?

When traveling, it pays to be prepared if illness strikes. To begin with, familiarize yourself with the parts of the body in Table 15.1.

Table 15.1 Parts of the Body

Body Part	Spanish	Pronunciation
ankle	el tobillo	ehl toh-bee-yoh
arm	el brazo	ehl brah-soh
back	la espalda	lah ehs-pahl-dah
body	el cuerpo	ehl kwehr-poh
brain	el cerebro	ehl seh-reh-broh
calf	la pantorrilla	lah pahn-toh-rree-yah
cheek	la mejilla	lah meh-hee-yah
chest	el pecho	ehl peh-choh
chin	la barbilla	lah bahr-bee-yah
ear	la oreja	lah oh-reh-hah
elbow	el codo	ehl koh-doh
eye	el ojo	ehl oh-hoh
face	la figura, la cara	lah fee-goo-rah, lah kah-rah
finger	el dedo	ehl deh-doh
foot	el pie	ehl pee-yeh
forehead	la frente	lah frehn-teh
gall bladder	la vejiga de la bilis	lah beh-hee-gah deh lah bee-lees
gland	la glándula	lah glahn-doo-lah
hair	el pelo	ehl peh-loh
hand	la mano	lah mah-noh
head	la cabeza	lah kah-beh-sah
heart	el corazón	ehl koh-rah-sohn
hip	la cadera	lah kah-deh-rah
kidney	el riñon	ehl rree-nyohn
knee	la rodilla	lah rroh-dee-yah

Body Part	Spanish	Pronunciation
leg	la pierna	lah pee-yehr-nah
lip	el labio	el lah-bee-yoh
liver	el hígado	ehl ee-gah-doh
lung	el pulmón	ehl pool-mohn
mouth	la boca	lah boh-kah
nail	la uña	lah oo-nyah
neck	el cuello	ehl kweh-yoh
nose	la nariz	lah nah-rees
skin	la piel	lah pee-yehl
shoulder	el hombro	ehl ohm-broh
spine	la espina	lah ehs-pee-nah
stomach	el estómago	ehl ehs-toh-mah-goh
throat	la garganta	lah gar-gahn-tah
toe	el dedo de pie	ehl deh-doh deh pee-yeh
tongue	la lengua	lah lehn-gwah
tooth	el diente	ehl dee-yehn-teh
wrist	la muñeca	lah moo-nyeh-kah

It Hurts Me Right Here

Do you want to avoid a trip to the doctor while on vacation? The best piece of advice anyone can give you is this: If you don't have a cast-iron stomach, don't drink tap water when you travel. Let's say you ignored this warning, however, because you truly believe Montezuma's Revenge (also known as severe diarrhea) is a thing of the past. You ate salad greens washed in tap water. Or you ordered a drink on the rocks, forgetting the future gastrointestinal effects the ice cubes might have. You've spent the better part of a day in *el baño* (the bathroom), and now you feel you must see a doctor. The obvious first question will be "What's the matter with you?" "*¿Qué le pasa?*" (keh leh pah-sah) To express what hurts or what bothers you, use the expression *tener dolor de (en)* + the part of the body.

I have a stomach ache.
Tengo dolor del estómago.
tehn-goh doh-lohr dehl ehs-toh-mah-goh

He has a pain in his foot.
Tiene dolor en el pie.
tee-yeh-neh doh-lohr ehn ehl pee-yeh

I have a toothache.
Tengo dolor de muelas.
tehn-goh doh-lohr deh mweh-lahs

What Are Your Symptoms?

Let's say your symptoms are more specific than a vague ache or pain. Table 15.2 provides a list of possible symptoms, which will come in handy if you need to describe a problem. Preface your complaint with "*Tengo ...*" (tehn-goh, I have ...).

Table 15.2 Other Symptoms

Symptom	Spanish	Pronunciation
abscess	un absceso	oon ahb-seh-soh
blister	una ampolla	oo-nah ahm-poh-yah
boil	un divieso	oon dee-bee-yeh-soh

Symptom	Spanish	Pronunciation
broken bone	un hueso roto	oon oo-eh-soh roh-toh
bruise	una contusión	oo-nah kohn-too-see-yohn
bump	una hinchazón	oo-nah een-chah-sohn
burn	una quemadura	oo-nah keh-mah-doo-rah
chills	escalofríos	oon ehs-kah-loh-free-yohs
cough	un tos	oon tohs
cramp	un calambre	oon kah-lahm-breh
cut	un corte	oon kohr-teh
diarrhea	una diarrea	oo-nah dee-yah-rreh-yah
fever	una fiebre	oo-nah fee-yeh-breh
fracture	una fractura	oo-nah frahk-too-rah
indigestion	una indigestión	oo-nah een-dee-hehs-tee-yohn
infection	una infección	oo-nah een-fehk-see-yohn
lump	un bulto	oon bool-toh
migraine	una jaqueca	oo-nah hah-keh-kah
pain	un dolor	oon doh-lohr
rash	una erupción	oo-nah eh-roop-see-yohn
sprain	una torcedura	oo-nah tohr-seh-doo-rah
swelling	una inflamación	oo-nah een-flah-mah-see-yohn
wound	un herido	oon eh-ree-doh

Here are some other phrases that might prove useful when explaining how you're feeling:

I'm coughing.	I'm sneezing.
Toso.	*Estornudo.*
toh-soh	ehs-tohr-noo-doh

I'm nauseous.
Tengo náuseas.
tehn-goh now-
seh-yahs

I'm bleeding.
Estoy sangrando.
ehs-toy sahn-grahn-
doh

I can't sleep.
No puedo dormir.
noh pweh-doh
dohr-meer

I'm exhausted.
Estoy agotado(a).
ehs-toy ah-goh-tah-
doh(dah)

I hurt everywhere.
Me duele todo el cuerpo.
meh dweh-leh toh-
doh ehl kwehr-poh

I feel bad.
Me siento mal.
meh see-yehn-toh
mahl

I'm dizzy.
Estoy mareado(a).
ehs-toy mah-reh-
yah-doh (dah)

I feel weak.
Me siento débil.
meh see-yehn-toh deh-
beel

Telling It Like It Is

The doctor might have to ask you many personal questions about your general overall health and family history. Be prepared—there also will be forms to complete. The doctor or nurse might ask you if you have some of the symptoms or illnesses listed in Table 15.3.

Have you had …?
¿Ha tenido …?
hah teh-nee-doh

Do you suffer from …?
¿Sufre de …?
soo-freh deh

Table 15.3   Other Symptoms and Illnesses

Illness	Spanish	Pronunciation
allergic reaction	una reacción alérgica	oo-nah rreh-ahk-see-yohn ah-lehr-hee-kah
appendicitis	la apendicitis	lah ah-pehn-dee-see-tees
asthma	la asma	lah ahs-mah
bronchitis	la bronquitis	lah brohn-kee-tees
cancer	el cáncer	ehl kahn-sehr
cold a chest cold a head cold	un resfriado un catarro del pecho el constipado	oon rrehs-free-yah-doh oon kah-tah-rroh dehl peh-choh ehl kohn-stee-pah-doh
diabetes	la diabetes	lah dee-yah-bee-tees
dizziness	el vértigo	ehl behr-tee-goh
exhaustion	la fatiga	lah fah-tee-gah
flu	la gripe	lah gree-peh
hay fever	la fiebre del heno	lah fee-yeh-breh dehl eh-noh
heart attack	un ataque de corazón	oon ah-tah-keh deh koh-rah-sohn
hepatitis	la hepatitis	lah eh-pah-tee-tees
measles	el sarampión	ehl sah-rahm-pee-yohn
mumps	las paperas	lahs pah-peh-rahs
pneumonia	la pulmonía	lah pool-moh-nee-yah
stroke	un ataque del apoplejía	oon ah-tah-keh dehl ah-poh-pleh-hee-yah
sunstroke	una insolación	oo-nah een-soh-lah-see-yohn

Remember to give the doctor any pertinent information that might help him serve you better. You might need some of the following phrases:

I've had this pain since …
Tengo este dolor desde …
tehn-goh ehs-teh doh-lohr dehs-deh

There's a (no) family history of …
(No) hay incidencia de … en mi familia.
(noh) ahy een-see-dehn-see-yah deh… ehn mee fah-meel-yah

I am (not) allergic to …
(No) soy alérgico(a) a …
(noh) soy ah-lehr-hee-koh(kah) ah

I had … … years ago.
Tuve … hace … años.
too-beh … ah-seh … ah-nyohs

I'm taking …
Tomo …
toh-moh

I'm pregnant.
Estoy embarazada.
ehs-toy ehm-bah-rah-sah-dah

Want to know how serious it is? Ask the following:

Is it serious?	Is it contagious?
¿Es serio (grave)?	*¿Es contagioso?*
ehs seh-ree-yoh (grah-beh)	ehs kohn-tah-hee-yoh-soh

How often must I take this medicine?
¿Cuántas veces al día tengo que tomar esta medicina?
kwahn-tahs beh-sehs ahl dee-yah tehn-goh keh
toh-mahr ehs-tah meh-dee-see-nah

How long do I have to stay in bed?
¿Cuánto tiempo tengo que quedarme en cama?
kwahn-toh tee-yehm-poh tehn-goh keh keh-
dahr-meh ehn kah-mah

May I please have a receipt for my medical
insurance?
¿Puede darme una quita para mi seguro médico?
pweh-deh dahr-meh oo-nah kee-tah pah-rah
mee seh-goo-roh meh-dee-koh

Explanations

You might find it necessary to explain how something happened.

I fell.	I cut myself.	I burned myself.
Me cayó.	*Me corté.*	*Me quemé.*
meh kah-yoh	meh kohr-teh	meh keh-meh

How Long Has This Been Going On?

Your doctor will probably ask how long you've been
experiencing your symptoms. Table 15.4 shows the
two ways you might hear the question posed and
shows how to answer each question.

Table 15.4 How Long Have Your Symptoms Lasted?

Question	Answer
¿Cuánto tiempo hace que + present tense of verb ...? kwahn-toh tee-yehm-poh ah-seh keh	Hace + time + que + present tense of the verb ah-seh... keh
¿Desde cuándo ... + present tense of verb? dehs-deh kwahn-doh	present tense of verb + desde hace + time
(For) How long have you been suffering? ¿Cuánto tiempo hace que Ud. sufre? kwahn-toh tee-yehm-poh ah-seh keh oo-stehd soo-freh	(I've been suffering) For two days. Hace dos días (que sufro). ah-seh dohs dee-yahs (keh soo-froh)
(For) How long have you been suffering? ¿Desde cuándo sufre Ud.? dehs-deh kwahn-doh soo-freh oo-stehd	(I've been suffering) Since yesterday. (Sufro) Desde hace ayer. (soo-froh) dehs-deh ah-seh ah-yehr

At the Pharmacy

In general, when traveling outside the United States, you should not expect to find a pharmacy that carries the wide range of supplies found in many of our drug stores: stationery, cards, cosmetics, candy, and household items. In the Spanish-speaking world, pharmacies are specifically health related. They often dispense medicines and drugs over the counter that would require a prescription in the States. Many large cities and towns have at least one all-night pharmacy called *una farmacia de guardia* (oo-nah fahr-mah-see-yah deh gwahr-dee-yah). If a drug store is closed, look on the door for a sign listing the nearest stores that are open.

If you are looking to restock your make-up kit or if you need a bottle of your favorite scent, you must go to *una perfumería* (oo-nah pehr-foo-meh-ree-yah), which specializes in toiletries.

If you are trying to find the closest drug store, you might want to ask:

> Where's the nearest (all-night) pharmacy?
> *¿Dónde está la farmacia (de guardia) más cercana?*
> dohn-deh ehs-tah lah fahr-mah-see-yah (deh gwahr-dee-yah) mahs sehr-kah-nah

When you speak to the druggist, you would say:

> I need medication.
> *Necesito medicina.*
> neh-seh-see-toh meh-dee-see-nah

> Could you please fill this prescription (immediately)?
> *¿Podría Ud. ejecutar esta receta (en seguida)?*
> poh-dree-yah oo-stehd eh-heh-koo-tahr ehs-tah rreh-seh-tah (ehn seh-gee-dah)

> How long will it take?
> *¿Cuánto tiempo tardará?*
> kwahn-toh tee-yehm-poh tahr-dah-rah

When you're simply looking for something over-the-counter, Table 15.5 will help you find it in the *farmacia*, the *perfumería*, or even the *supermercado*. Tell the clerk "*Busco...*" (boos-koh, I'm looking for...) or "*Necesito...*" (neh-seh-see-toh, I need).

Table 15.5 Drugstore Items

Item	Spanish	Pronunciation
For Men and Women		
alcohol	el alcohol	ehl ahl-koh-ohl
antacid	un antiácido	oon ahn-tee-ah-see-doh
antihistamine	un antistamínico	oon ahn-tee-stah-mee-nee-koh
antiseptic	un antiséptico	oon ahn-tee-sehp-tee-koh
aspirin	las aspirinas	lahs ahs-pee-ree-nahs
bandage	una venda	oo-nah behn-dah
Band-aid	una curita	oo-nah koo-ree-tah
brush	un cepillo	oon seh-pee-yoh
comb	un peine	oon peh-ee-neh
condoms	los condones	lohs kohn-doh-nehs
cotton (absorbent)	el algodón hidrófilo	ehl ahl-goh-dohn ee-droh-fee-loh
cough drops	las pastillas para la tos	lahs pahs-tee-yahs pah-rah lah tohs
cough syrup	el jarabe para la tos	ehl hah-rah-beh pah-rah lah tohs
deodorant	el desodorante	ehl deh-soh-doh-rahn-teh
ear drops	las gotas para los oídos	lahs goh-tahs pah-rah lohs oh-ee-dohs
eye drops	las gotas para los ojos	lahs goh-tahs pah-rah lohs oh-hohs

Item	Spanish	Pronunciation
first-aid kit	un botiquín de primeros auxilios	oon boh-tee-keen deh pree-meh-rohs owk-see-lee-yohs
gel	la gomina, la gelatina	lah goh-mee-nah, lah heh-lah-tee-nah
hair spray	la laca	lah lah-kah
heating pad	la almohadilla de califacción	lah ahl-moh-ah-dee-yah deh kah-lee-fahk-see-yohn
ice pack	una bolsa de hielo	oo-nah bohl-sah deh ee-yeh-loh
laxative (mild)	un laxante (ligero)	oon lahk-sahn-teh (lee-heh-roh)
milk of magnesia	la leche de magnesia	lah leh-cheh deh mahg-nee-see-yah
mirror	un espejo	oon ehs-peh-hoh
moisturizer	la crema hidratante	lah kreh-mah ee-drah-tahn-teh
mousse	la espuma	lah ehs-poo-mah
mouthwash	un elixir bucal	oon eh-leek-seer boo-kahl
nail file	una lima	oo-nah lee-mah
nail-clippers	el cortauñas	ehl kohr-tah-oo-nyahs
nose drops	las gotas para la nariz	lahs goh-tahs pah-rah lah nah-rees
pills	las pastillas	lahs pahs-tee-yahs
razor (electric)	la maquinilla de afeitar (eléctica)	lah mah-kee-nee-yah deh ah-feh-ee-tahr (eh-lehk-tee-kah)
razor blade	la hoja de afeitar	lah oh-hah deh ah-feh-ee-tahr

continues

Table 15.5 (continued)

Item	Spanish	Pronunciation
safety pin	el seguro, el imperdible	ehl seh-goo-roh, ehl eem-pehr-dee-bleh
scissors	las tijeras	lahs tee-heh-rahs
shampoo (anti-dandruff)	el champú (anti-caspa)	ehl chahm-poo (ahn-tee kahs-pah)
shaving cream	la crema de afeitar	lah kreh-mah deh ah-feh-ee-tahr
sleeping pills	las pastillas para dormir	lahs pahs-tee-yahs pah-rah dohr-meer
soap (bar)	el jabón (una pastilla de jabón)	ehl hah-bohn (oo-nah pahs-tee-yah deh hah-bohn)
sponge	una esponja	oo-nah ehs-pohn-hah
suntan lotion	bronceador	brohn-seh-yah-dohr
talcum powder	los polvos de talco	lohs pohl-bohs deh tahl-koh
thermometer	un termómetro	oon tehr-moh-meh-troh
tissues	los pañuelos de papel	lohs pah-nyoo-weh-lohs deh pah-pehl
toilet paper	el papel higiénico	ehl pah-pehl ee-hee-eh-nee-koh
toothbrush	el cepillo de los dientes	ehl seh-pee-yoh deh lohs dee-yehn-tehs
toothpaste	la pasta dentifrica	lah pahs-tah dehn-tee-free-kah
vitamins	las vitaminas	lahs bee-tah-mee-nahs
For Men Only		
after-shave lotion	la loción facial	lah loh-see-yohn fah-see-yahl
cologne	la colonia	lah koh-loh-nee-yah

Item	Spanish	Pronunciation
For Women Only		
blush	el colorete de mejillas	ehl koh-loh-reh-teh deh meh-hee-yahs
bobby pins	los pasadores	lohs pah-sah-doh-rehs
cleansing cream	un demaquill-ador, la loción, la leche desma-quilladora	oon deh-mah-kee-yah-dohr, lah loh-see-yohn, lah leh-cheh dehs-mah-kee-yah-doh-rah
emery boards	las limas	lahs lee-mahs
eye liner	el lápiz de ojos	ehl lah-pees deh oh-hohs
eyebrow pencil	el lápiz de cejas	ehl lah-pees deh seh-hahs
eye shadow	la sombra de ojos	lah sohm-brah deh oh-hohs
foundation	la crema, la base	lah kreh-mah, lah bah-seh
lipstick	el lápiz, la barra de labios	ehl lah-pees, lah bah-rrah deh lah-bee-yohs
makeup	el maquillaje	ehl mah-kee-yah-heh
mascara	el rímel	ehl rree-mehl
nail polish	el esmalte	ehl ehs-mahl-teh
nail polish remover	el quitaesmaltes	ehl kee-tah-ehs-mahl-tehs
perfume	el perfume	ehl pehr-foo-meh
powder	los polvos	lohs pohl-bohs
rouge	el colorete	ehl koh-loh-reh-teh
sanitary napkins	las toallas higiénicas	lahs toh-wah-yahs ee-hee-eh-nee-kahs
tampons	los tampones	lohs tahm-poh-nehs

continues

Table 15.5 (continued)

Item	Spanish	Pronunciation
	For Babies	
bottle	un biberón	oon bee-beh-rohn
diapers (disposable)	los pañales (desechables)	lohs pah-nyah-lehs (deh-seh-chah-blehs)
pacifier	un chupete	oon choo-peh-teh

Special Items

A pharmacy that specializes in *el alquiler de aparatos médicos* (ehl ahl-kee-lehr deh ah-pah-rah-tohs meh-dee-kohs)—the rental of medical appliances—would either sell or have information about the items for the physically challenged featured in Table 15.6.

> Where can I get ...?
> *¿Dónde puedo obtener ...?*
> dohn-deh pweh-doh ohb-teh-nehr

Table 15.6 Special Needs

Item	Spanish	Pronunciation
cane	un bastón	oon bahs-tohn
crutches	las muletas	lahs moo-leh-tahs
hearing aid	un aparato para sordos	oon ah-pah-rah-toh pah-rah sohr-dohs
walker	un andador	oon ahn-dah-dohr
wheelchair	una silla, un sillón de ruedas	oo-nah see-yah, oon see-yohn deh rroo-weh-dahs

16

Business as Usual

In This Chapter

- How to make a phone call
- Dealing with your mail
- Stationery store supplies
- Faxes and computers

Conducting business in a foreign country is always a bit of a challenge. It's crucial to understand how to place a phone call, send a letter, buy necessary stationery supplies, and deal with faxes. Being computer literate in any language is probably one of the most important skills you'll need to possess. This chapter will help you deal with all of this.

If you plan to call long distance from a foreign country, whether for business or for pleasure, expect that someone will have to explain how to use the local phone system. It is also likely that the procedures for making local calls will be different from what you are used to back home. You will want to make sure to correctly express the type of call you want to make. Table 16.1 provides you with some options.

Table 16.1 Types of Phone Calls

Type of Call	Spanish	Pronunciation
collect call	una llamada por cobrar, una llamada con cargo	oo-nah yah-mah-dah pohr koh-brahr, oo-nah yah-mah-dah kohn kahr-goh
credit-card call	una llamada con tarjeta de crédito	oo-nah yah-mah-dah kohn tahr-heh-tah deh kreh-dee-toh
local call	una llamada local	oo-nah yah-mah-dah loh-kahl
long-distance call	una llamada de larga distancia	oo-nah yah-mah-dah deh lahr-gah dees-tahn-see-yah
out-of-the-country call	una llamada internacional	oo-nah yah-mah-dah een-tehr-nah-see-yohn-nahl

Table 16.2 provides the words to help you understand Spanish directions for placing a phone call.

Table 16.2 How to Make a Phone Call

Action	Spanish	Pronunciation
to call	telefonear, llamar por teléfono	teh-leh-foh-neh-yahr, lah-mahr pohr teh-leh-foh-noh
to call back	volver(ue) a llamar	bohl-behr ah yah-mahr
to dial	marcar	mahr-kahr
to hang up (the receiver)	colgar	kohl-gahr
to insert the card	introducir la tarjeta	een-troh-doo-seer lah tahr-heh-tah

Action	Spanish	Pronunciation
to know the area code	saber la clave de área	sah-behr lah klah-beh deh ah-reh-yah
to leave a message	dejar un mensaje	de-hahr oon mehn-sah-heh
to make a call	hacer una llamada	ah-sehr oo-nah yah-mah-dah
to pick up (the receiver)	descolgar	dehs-kohl-gahr
to telephone	telefonear	teh-leh-foh-neh-yahr
to wait for the dial tone	esperar el tono, la señal	ehs-peh-rahr ehl toh-noh, lah seh-nyahl

Problems

Are you having trouble reaching your party? The following are some phrases you might say or hear when you are having problems:

What number are you calling?
¿Qué número está Ud. llamando?
keh noo-meh-roh ehs-tah oo-stehd yah-mahn-doh

(I have) You have the wrong number.
(Yo tengo) Ud. tiene un número equivocado.
yoh teh-goh (oo-stehd tee-yeh-neh) oon noo-meh-roh eh-kee-boh-kah-doh

We got cut off (disconnected).
Se nos cortó la línea.
seh nohs kohr-toh lah lee-neh-yah

Please redial the number.
Remarque Ud. el número, por favor.
rreh-mahr-keh oo-stehd ehl noo-meh-roh pohr
fah-bohr

The telephone is out of order.
*El teleféno está descompuesto (dañado, fuera de
servicio).*
ehl teh-leh-foh-noh ehs-tah dehs-kohm-pwehs-toh
(dah-nyah-doh, fweh-rah deh sehr-bee-see-yoh)

There's a lot of static on the line.
Hay muchos parásitos (mucha estática) en la línea.
ahy moo-chohs pah-rah-see-tohs (moo-chah ehs-
tah-tee-kah) ehn lah lee-neh-yah

I'll Write, Instead

It's far more cost effective to send a letter than to
place a long-distance call. Table 16.3 provides the
vocabulary you need to send your mail.

Table 16.3 Mail and Post Office Terms

Term	Spanish	Pronunciation
address	la dirección	lah dee-rehk-see-yohn
addressee	el destinatario	ehl dehs-tee-nah-tah-ree-yoh
air letter	el correo aéreo	ehl koh-rreh-yoh ah-eh-reh-yoh
envelope	el sobre	ehl soh-breh
letter	la carta	lah kahr-tah

Term	Spanish	Pronunciation
mailbox	el buzón	ehl boo-sohn
package	el paquete	ehl pah-keh-teh
post card	la tarjeta postal	lah tahr-heh-tah pohs-tahl
postage	el franqueo	ehl frahn-keh-yoh
postal code	el código postal	ehl koh-dee-goh pohs-tahl
postal worker	el cartero (la cartera)	ehl kahr-teh-roh (lah kahr-teh-rah)
rate	la tarifa de franqueo	lah tah-ree-fah deh frahn-keh-yoh
sheet of stamps	la hoja de sellos	lah oh-hah deh seh-yohs
stamp	el sello	ehl seh-yoh

If you just need stamps, save time and pick them up at *estancos* (ehs-tahn-kohs), which are authorized to sell tobacco, stamps, and seals. When you're ready to send a letter or post card home, look for the red and yellow mailboxes.

Getting Service

You've written your letter, folded it, and sealed it in an envelope. All you need to do is find a post office or a mailbox. If you don't know where one is located, simply ask:

Where is the nearest post office (mailbox)?
¿Dónde está el correos (el buzón) más próximo?
dohn-deh ehs-tah ehl koh-reh-yohs (ehl boo-sohn) mahs prohk-see-moh

Different types of letters and packages require special forms, paperwork, and special postage rates. It is important to know how to ask for the type of service you need.

What is the postage rate for …?
¿Cuál es la tarifa de franqueo de …?
kwahl ehs lah tah-ree-fah deh frahn-keh-yoh deh

Phrase	Spanish	Pronunciation
an insured letter	una carta asegurada	oo-nah kahr-tah ah-seh-goo-rah-dah
a letter to the United States	una carta a los Estados Unidos	oo-nah kahr-tah ah lohs ehs-tah-dohs oo-nee-dohs
an air-mail letter	una carta por correo aéreo	oo-nah kahr-tah pohr koh-rreh-yoh ah-ee-ree-yoh
a registered letter	una carta certificada	oo-nah kahr-tah sehr-tee-fee-kah-dah
a special-delivery letter	una carta urgente	oo-nah kahr-tah oor-hehn-teh

I would like to send this letter (this package) by regular mail (by air mail, special delivery).
Quiero mandar esta carta (este paquete) por correo regular (aéreo, urgente).
kee-yeh-roh mahn-dahr ehs-tah kahr-tah (ehs-teh pah-keh-teh) pohr koh-rreh-yoh rreh-goo-lahr (ah-eh-reh-yoh, oor-gehn-teh)

How much does this letter (package) weigh?
¿Cuánto pesa esta carta (este paquete)?
kwahn-toh peh-sah ehs-tah kahr-tah (ehs-teh
pah-keh-teh)

When will it arrive?
¿Cuándo llegaré (llegarán)?
kwahn-doh yeh-gah-reh (yeh-gah-rahn)

I Need Supplies

To successfully conduct any type of business, it is
necessary to keep certain basic supplies on hand. No
doubt, you'll want to stop at *la papelería* (lah pah-peh-
leh-ree-yah), the stationery store, to stock up on the
business items listed in Table 16.4. Start by saying:

I would like to buy ...
Quisiera comprar ...
kee-see-yeh-rah kohm-prahr

Table 16.4   At the Stationery Store

Supply	Spanish	Pronunciation
ball-point pen	un bolígrafo	oon boh-lee-grah-foh
calculator (solar)	una calculadora (solar)	oo-nah kahl-koo-lah-doh-rah (soh-lahr)
envelopes	unos sobres	oo-nohs soh-brehs
eraser	una goma	oo-nah goh-mah
glue	el pegamento	ehl peh-gah-mehn-toh
notebook	un cuaderno	oon kwah-dehr-noh
paper	un papel	oon pah-pehl

continues

Table 16.4 (continued)

Supply	Spanish	Pronunciation
paper clips	unos sujeta-papeles	oo-nohs soo-heh-tah-pah-peh-lehs
pencils	unos lápices	oo-nohs lah-pee-sehs
pencil sharpener	un sacapuntas	oon sah-kah-poon-tahs
Post-its	unas notas autoadhesivas desprendibles	oo-nahs noh-tahs ow-toh-ahd-eh-see-bahs dehs-prehn-dee-blehs
ruler	una regla	oo-nah rreh-glah
scotch tape	una cinta adhesiva	oo-nah seen-tah ahd-eh-see-bah
stapler	una grapadora	oo-nah grah-pah-doh-rah
stationery	unos objetos de escritorio	oo-nohs ohb-heh-tohs deh ehs-kree-toh-ree-yoh
string	una cuerda	oo-nah kwehr-dah
wrapping paper	un papel del envoltorio	oon pah-pehl dehl ehn-bol-toh-ree-yoh
writing pad	un bloc	oon blohk

Fax It

Let's face it, a fax machine is becoming almost as important as a telephone in many households. When you can transmit and receive messages and information in a matter of seconds or minutes, you can speed up the time it takes to transact business. That translates into extra cash. If you are conducting business in a Spanish-speaking country, it's a must to be fax-literate.

Do you have a fax machine?
¿Tiene Ud. un fax?
tee-yeh-neh oo-stehd oon fahks

What is your fax number?
¿Cuál es su número de fax?
kwahl ehs soo noo-meh-roh deh fahks

I'd like to send a fax.
Quisiera mandar un fax.
kee-see-yeh-rah mahn-dahr oon fahks

Fax it to me.
Enviémelo por fax.
ehn-bee-yeh-meh-loh pohr fahks

I didn't get your fax.
Yo no recibí (Yo no he recibido) su fax.
yoh noh rreh-see-bee (yoh noh eh rreh-see-bee-doh) soo fahks

Did you receive my fax?
¿Recibió (¿Ha recibido) Ud. mi fax?
rreh-see-bee-yoh (ah rreh-see-bee-doh) oo-stehd mee fahks

I'm a Computer Geek

Today a computer is an absolute necessity. You must know enough about the industry standards and programs for your field of work as well as for the system you are using. The phrases that follow will help you, even if you're not a computer geek.

What kind of computer do you have?

¿Qué sistema (tipo, género) de computadora tiene Ud.?

keh sees-teh-mah (tee-poh, heh-neh-roh) deh
kohm-poo-tah-doh-rah tee-yeh-neh oo-stehd

What operating system are you using?

¿Qué sistema operador usa Ud. (está Ud. usando)?

keh sees-teh-mah oh-peh-rah-dohr oo-sah oo-
stehd (ehs-tah oo-stehd oo-sahn-doh)

What word-processing program are you using?

¿Qué procesador de textos usa Ud. (está Ud. usando)?

keh proh-seh-sah-dohr deh tehks-tohs oo-sah
oo-stehd (ehs-tah oo-stehd oo-sahn-doh)

What peripherals do you have?

¿Qué periféricos usa Ud. (está Ud. usando)?

keh peh-ree-feh-ree-kohs oo-sah oo-stehd
(ehs-tah oo-stehd oo-sahn-doh)

Are our systems compatible?

¿Son compatibles nuestros sistemas?

sohn kohm-pah-tee-blehs nwehs-trohs
sees-teh-mahs

Something Extra

To say Internet, use the term *el internet*
(ehl een-tehr-neht).

To speak about e-mail, you would use the
term *el correo electrónico* (ehl koh-rreh-yoh
eh-lehk-troh-nee-koh).

Verb Charts

Regular Verbs

-ar Verbs

usar, to use

Gerund: usando

Past participle: usado

Commands: ¡Use Ud.!, ¡Usen Uds.!, ¡Usemos!

Subj.	Present (do)	Subj.	Present (do)
yo	us**o**	nos.	us**amos**
tú	us**as**	vos.	us**áis**
él	us**a**	ellos	us**an**
Subjunctive: use, uses, use, usemos, uséis, usen			

-er Verbs

comer, to eat

Gerund: comiendo

Past participle: comido

Commands: ¡Coma Ud.!, ¡Coman Uds.!, ¡Comamos!

Subj.	Present	Subj.	Present
yo	como	nos.	comemos
tú	comes	vos.	coméis
él	come	ellos	comen

Subjunctive: coma, comas, coma, comamos, comáis, coman

-ir Verbs

vivir, to live

Gerund: viviendo

Past participle: vivido

Commands: ¡Viva Ud.!, ¡Vivan Uds.!, ¡Vivamos!

Subj.	Present	Subj.	Present
yo	vivo	nos.	vivimos
tú	vives	vos.	vivís
él	vive	ellos	viven

Subjunctive: viva, vivas, viva, vivamos, viváis, vivan

Irregular Verbs

dar, to give

Subj.	Present	Preterite
yo	doy	di
tú	das	diste

Subj.	Present	Preterite
él	da	dio
nos.	damos	dimos
vos.	dais	disteis
ellos	dan	dieron

Subjunctive: dé, des, dé, demos, deis, den

decir, to say

Gerund: diciendo

Past participle: dicho

Subj.	Present	Pret.	Future	Cond.
yo	digo	dije	diré	diría
tú	dices	dijiste	dirás	dirías
él	dice	dijo	dirá	diría
nos.	decimos	dijmos	diremos	diríamos
vos.	decís	dijisteis	diréis	diríais
ellos	dicen	dijeron	dirán	dirían

Subjunctive: diga, digas, diga, digamos, digáis, digan

estar, to be

Subj.	Present	Preterite
yo	estoy	estuve
tú	estás	estuviste
él	está	estuvo
nos.	estamos	estuvimos
vos.	estáis	estuvisteis
ellos	están	estuvieron

Subjunctive: esté, estés, esté, estemos, estéis, estén

hacer, to make, to do

Past participle: hecho

Subj.	Present	Pret.	Future	Cond.
yo	hago	hice	haré	haría
tú	haces	hiciste	harás	harías
él	hace	hizo	hará	haría
nos.	hacemos	hicimos	haremos	haríamos
vos.	hacéis	hicisteis	haréis	haríais
ellos	hacen	hicieron	harán	harían
Subjunctive: haga, hagas, haga, hagamos, hagáis, hagan				

ir, to go

Gerund: yendo

Subj.	Present	Preterite	Imperfect
yo	voy	fui	iba
tú	vas	fuiste	ibas
él	va	fue	iba
nos.	vamos	fuimos	íbamos
vos.	vais	fuisteis	ibais
ellos	van	fueron	iban
Subjunctive: vaya, vayas, vaya, vayamos, vayáis, vayan			

poder (o to ue), to be able to, can

Gerund: pudiendo

Subj.	Present	Pret.	Future	Cond.
yo	puedo	pude	podré	podría
tú	puedes	pudiste	podrás	podrías

Subj.	Present	Pret.	Future	Cond.
él	puede	pudo	podrá	podría
nos.	podemos	pudimos	podremos	podríamos
vos.	podéis	pudisteis	podréis	podríais
ellos	pueden	pudieron	podrán	podrían

Subjunctive: pueda, puedas, pueda, podamos, podáis, puedan

poner, to put, to place

Past participle: puesto

Subj.	Present	Pret.	Future	Cond.
yo	pongo	puse	pondré	pondría
tú	pones	pusiste	pondrás	pondrías
él	pone	puso	pondrá	pondría
nos.	ponemos	pusimos	pondremos	pondríamos
vos.	ponéis	pusisteis	pondréis	pondríais
ellos	ponen	pusieron	pondrán	pondrían

Subjunctive: ponga, pongas, ponga, pongamos, pongáis, pongan

querer, to want

Subj.	Present	Pret.	Future	Cond.
yo	quiero	quise	querré	querría
tú	quieres	quisiste	querrás	querrías
él	quiere	quiso	querrá	querría
nos.	queremos	quisimos	querremos	querríamos
vos.	queréis	quisisteis	querréis	querríais

continues

continued

Subj.	Present	Pret.	Future	Cond.
ellos	quieren	quisieron	querrán	querrían

Subjunctive: quiera, quieras, quiera, queramos, queráis, quieran

saber, to know

Subj.	Present	Pret.	Future	Cond.
yo	sé	supe	sabré	sabría
tú	sabes	supiste	sabrás	sabrías
él	sabe	supo	sabrá	sabría
nos.	sabemos	supimos	sabremos	sabríamos
vos.	sabéis	supisteis	sabréis	sabríais
ellos	saben	supieron	sabrán	sabrían

Subjunctive: sepa, sepas, sepa, sepamos, sepáis, sepan

salir, to go out

Subj.	Present	Future	Cond.
yo	salgo	saldré	saldría
tú	sales	saldrás	saldrías
él	sale	saldrá	saldría
nos.	salemos	saldremos	saldríamos
vos.	saléis	saldréis	saldríais
ellos	salen	saldrán	saldrían

Subjunctive: salga, salgas, salga, salgamos, salgáis, salgan

ser, to be

Subj.	Present	Pret.	Imperfect
yo	soy	fui	era
tú	eres	fuiste	eras
él	es	fue	era
nos.	somos	fuimos	éramos
vos.	sois	fuisteis	erais
ellos	son	fueron	eran

Subjunctive: sea, seas, sea, seamos, seáis, sean

tener, to have

Subj.	Present	Pret.	Future	Cond.
yo	tengo	tuve	tendré	tendría
tú	tienes	tuviste	tendrás	tendrías
él	tiene	tuvo	tendrá	tendría
nos.	tenemos	tuvimos	tendremos	tendríamos
vos.	tenéis	tuvisteis	tendréis	tendríais
ellos	tienen	tuvieron	tendrán	tendrían

Subjunctive: tenga, tengas, tenga, tengamos, tengáis, tengan

traer, to bring

Past participle: traído

Subj.	Present	Preterite
yo	traigo	traje
tú	traes	trajiste
él	trae	trajo
nos.	traemos	trajimos

continues

continued

Subj.	Present	Preterite
vos.	traéis	trajisteis
ellos	traen	trajeron

Subjunctive: traiga, traigas, traiga, traigamos, traigáis, traigan

venir, to come
Gerund: viniendo

Subj.	Present	Pret.	Future	Cond.
yo	vengo	vine	vendré	vendría
tú	vienes	viniste	vendrás	vendrías
él	viene	vino	vendrá	vendría
nos.	venimos	vinimos	vendremos	vendríamos
vos.	venís	vinisteis	vendréis	vendríais
ellos	vienen	vinieron	vendrán	vendrían

Subjunctive: venga, vengas, venga, vengamos, vengáis, vengan

ver, to see
Past participle: visto

Subj.	Present	Preterite	Imperfect
yo	veo	vi	veía
tú	ves	viste	veías
él	ve	vio	veía
nos.	vemos	vimos	veíamos
vos.	veis	visteis	veíais
ellos	ven	vieron	veían

Subjunctive: vea, veas, vea, veamos, veáis, vean

Spanish–English Dictionary

This dictionary follows international alphabetical order. The Spanish letter combination *ch* and *ll* are not treated as separate letters; therefore, *ch* will follow *cg* instead of being at the end of *c*, and *ll* will appear after *lk* and not at the end of *l*. Note that *ñ* is treated as a separate letter and follows *n* in alphabetical order.

Spanish	Pronunciation	English
a	ah	at, to
abrigo (m.)	ah-bree-goh	overcoat
abril	ah-breel	April
abrir	ah-breer	to open
aceite (m.)	ah-seh-yee-teh	oil
aduana (f.)	ah-doo-wah-nah	customs
advertir	ahd-behr-teer	to warn
agosto	ah-gohs-toh	August
agua (m.)	ah-gwah	water
ahora	ah-oh-rah	now
ahorrar	ah-oh-rrahr	to save
ajo (m.)	ah-hoh	garlic
alegre	ah-leh-greh	happy
algodón (m.)	ahl-goh-dohn	cotton

Spanish	Pronunciation	English
allá	ah-yah	there
almacén (m.)	ahl-mah-sehn	department store
alquilar	ahl-kee-lahr	to rent
alto	ahl-toh	tall
amarillo	ah-mah-ree-yoh	yellow
anaranjado	ah-nah-rahn-hah-doh	orange
anillo (m.)	ah-nee-yoh	ring
antes (de)	ahn-tehs (deh)	before
aprender	ah-prehn-dehr	to learn
aquí	ah-kee	here
arreglar	ah-rreh-glahr	to adjust, to fix
arroz (m.)	ah-rrohs	rice
asado	ah-sah-doh	baked, roasted
ascensor (m.)	ah-sehn-sohr	elevator
así	ah-see	so, thus
asiento (m.)	ah-see-yehn-toh	seat
aterrizar	ah-teh-rree-sahr	to land
avión (m.)	ah-bee-yohn	airplane
aviso (m.)	ah-bee-soh	warning
ayer	ah-yehr	yesterday
ayudar	ah-yoo-dahr	to help
azúcar (m.)	ah-soo-kahr	sugar
azul	ah-sool	blue
bajo	bah-hoh	short
banco (m.)	bahn-koh	bank
baño (m.)	bah-nyoh	bathroom
bastante	bahs-tahn-teh	enough, quite
basura (f.)	bah-soo-rah	garbage

Spanish	Pronunciation	English
beber	beh-behr	to drink
bien	byehn	well
bienvenido	byehn-beh-nee-doh	welcome
blanco	blahn-koh	white
boleto (m.)	boh-leh-toh	ticket
bolsa (f.)	bohl-sah	pocketbook
bonito	boh-nee-toh	pretty
botella (f.)	boh-teh-yah	bottle
bueno	bweh-noh	good
buscar	boos-kahr	to look for
buzón (m.)	boo-sohn	mailbox
caja fuerte (f.)	kah-hah fwehr-teh	safe, safe deposit box
cajero automático (m.)	kah-heh-roh ow-toh-mah-tee-koh	automatic teller machine
cama (f.)	kah-mah	bed
camarero(a)	kah-mah-reh-roh(rah)	waiter(ress)
cambiar	kahm-bee-yahr	to change
cambio de dinero (m.)	kahm-bee-yoh deh dee-neh-roh	money exchange
camisa (f.)	kah-mee-sah	shirt
carne (f.)	kahr-neh	meat
carta (f.)	kahr-tah	letter, menu, card
cerca (de)	sehr-kah (deh)	near
césped (m.)	sehs-pehd	lawn
chaleco salvavidas (m.)	chah-leh-koh sahl-bah-bee-dahs	life vest
champú (m.) anti-caspa	chahm-poo ahn-tee kahs-pah	shampoo anti-dandruff

Spanish	Pronunciation	English
ciento	see-yehn-toh	hundred
cinco (m.)	seen-koh	five
cincuenta	seen-kwehn-tah	fifty
cine (m.)	see-neh	movies
cinturón de seguridad (m.)	seen-too-rohn deh seh-goo-ree-dahd	seat belt
claro	klah-roh	light, of course
coche (m.)	koh-cheh	car
collar (m.)	koh-yahr	necklace
comenzar	koh-mehn-sahr	to begin
comer	koh-mehr	to eat
comisaria de policia (f.)	koh-mee-sah-ree-yah deh poh-lee-see-yah	police station
cómo	koh-moh	how
comprar	kohm-prahr	to buy, to purchase
comprender	kohm-prehn-dehr	to understand
con	kohn	with
contestar	kohn-tehs-tahr	to answer
contra	kohn-trah	against
corbata (f.)	kohr-bah-tah	tie
creer	kreh-ehr	to believe
cruzar	kroo-sar	to cross
cuál	kwahl	which
cuándo	kwahn-doh	when
cuánto	kwahn-toh	how much, many
cuarenta	kwah-rehn-tah	forty
cuatro	kwah-troh	four
cubierto	koo-bee-yehr-toh	overcast
dar	dahr	to give

Spanish	Pronunciation	English
de	deh	about, from, of
de nada	deh nah-dah	you're welcome
de nuevo	deh nweh-boh	again
debajo de	deh-bah-hoh deh	below, beneath, under
deber + infinitive	deh-behr	to have to + infinitive
decir	deh-seer	to say, to tell
delante de	deh-lahn-teh deh	in front of
demasiado	deh-mah-see-yah-doh	too much
desde	dehs-deh	from, since
después (de)	dehs-pwehs (deh)	after
detrás de	deh-trahs deh	behind
día (m.)	dee-yah	day
diciembre	dee-see-yehm-breh	December
diez	dee-yehs	ten
dinero (m.)	dee-neh-roh	currency, money
dirección (f.)	dee-rehk-see-yohn	address
doblar	doh-blahr	to turn
doce	doh-seh	twelve
domingo	doh-meen-goh	Sunday
dónde	dohn-deh	where
dos	dohs	two
durante	doo-rahn-teh	during
empleado (m.)	ehm-pleh-yah-doh	employee
en	ehn	in
en seguida	ehn seh-gee-dah	immediately
enero	eh-neh-roh	January
enfermo	ehn-fehr-moh	sick

Spanish	Pronunciation	English
enfrente de	ehn-frehn-teh deh	in front of
entender	ehn-tehn-dehr	to understand
entre	ehn-treh	among, between
enviar	ehn-bee-yahr	to send
escribir	ehs-kree-beer	to write
escuchar	ehs-koo-char	to listen to
esperar	ehs-peh-rahr	to hope, to wait for, to wish
Estados Unidos (m./pl.)	ehs-tah-dohs oo-nee-dohs	United States
estar	ehs-tahr	to be
este (m.)	ehs-teh	East
febrero	feh-breh-roh	February
firmar	feer-mahr	to sign
franqueo (m.)	frahn-keh-yoh	postage
frente a	frehn-teh ah	facing, opposite
fuera de servicio	fweh-rah deh sehr-bee-see-yoh	out of order
ganar	gah-nahr	to earn, to win
gerente (m.)	heh-rehn-teh	manager
gobernanta (f.)	goh-behr-nahn-tah	maid service
grande	grahn-deh	big
gustar	goos-tahr	to like
hablar	hah-blahr	to speak, to talk
hacer	ah-sehr	to do, to make
hacia	ah-see-yah	toward
hasta	ahs-tah	until
helado (m.)	eh-lah-doh	ice cream
hola	oh-lah	hello

Spanish	Pronunciation	English
hora (f.)	oh-rah	hour, time
hoy	oy	today
huevo	weh-boh	egg
iglesia (f.)	ee-gleh-see-yah	church
impermeable (m.)	eem-pehr-meh-yah-bleh	raincoat
invierno (m.)	een-bee-yehr-noh	winter
ir	eer	to go
jefe (m.)	heh-feh	department head
joven	hoh-behn	young
joya (f.)	hoh-yah	jewel
jueves	hweh-behs	Thursday
julio	hoo-lee-yoh	July
junio	hoo-nee-yoh	June
lápiz (m.)	lah-pees	pencil
largo	lahr-goh	long
lavable	lah-bah-bleh	washable
lavandería (f.)	lah-bahn-deh-ree-yah	laundry and dry cleaning service
leche (f.)	leh-cheh	milk
leer	leh-ehr	to read
lejos (de)	leh-hohs (deh)	far (from)
libro (m.)	lee-broh	book
listo	lees-toh	ready
llave (f.)	yah-beh	key
llegar	yeh-gahr	to arrive
lugar (m.)	loo-gahr	place
lunes	loo-nehs	Monday
madre (f.)	mah-dreh	mother

Spanish	Pronunciation	English
maíz (m.)	mah-yees	corn
maleta (f.)	mah-leh-tah	suitcase
malo	mah-loh	bad
mandar	mahn-dahr	to order, to send
mano (f.)	mah-noh	hand
mantequilla (f.)	mahn-teh-kee-yah	butter
manzana (f.)	mahn-sah-nah	apple
mañana	mah-nyah-nah	tomorrow, morning
marca (f.)	mahr-kah	brand name
martes	mahr-tehs	Tuesday
marzo	mahr-soh	March
más	mahs	more
mayo	mah-yoh	May
medio	meh-dee-yoh	half
mejor	meh-hohr	better
menos	meh-nohs	less
mensaje (m.)	mehn-sah-heh	message
mercado (m.)	mehr-kah-doh	market
mes (m.)	mehs	month
mesa (f.)	meh-sah	table
metro (m.)	meh-troh	subway
mezclar	mehs-klahr	to mix
miércoles	mee-yehr-koh-lehs	Wednesday
mil	meel	thousand
mirar	mee-rahr	to look at, to watch
moneda (f.)	moh-neh-dah	coin
montaña (f.)	mohn-tah-nyah	mountain

Spanish	Pronunciation	English
montar	mohn-tahr	to go up, to ride
mostrador (m.)	mohs-trah-dohr	counter
mucho	moo-choh	much, many
muebles (m. pl.)	mweh-blehs	furniture
museo (m.)	moo-seh-yoh	museum
muy	mwee	very
nadie	nah-dee-yeh	nobody
naranja (f.)	nah-rahn-hah	orange
negro	neh-groh	black
noche (f.)	noh-cheh	evening
norte (m.)	nohr-teh	North
noticias (f./pl.)	noh-tee-see-yahs	news
noventa	noh-behn-tah	ninety
novio(a)	noh-bee-yoh(yah)	boy(girl)friend
noviembre	noh-bee-yehm-breh	November
nueve	nweh-beh	nine
nuevo	nweh-boh	new
ochenta	oh-chen-tah	eighty
ocho	oh-choh	eight
octubre	ohk-too-breh	October
oeste (m.)	oh-ehs-teh	West
oír	oh-eer	to hear
ojo (m.)	oh-hoh	eye
once	ohn-seh	eleven
ordinador (m.)	ohr-dee-nah-dohr	computer
oro (m.)	oh-roh	gold
otoño (m.)	oh-toh-nyoh	autumn
padre (m.)	pah-dreh	father

Spanish	Pronunciation	English
pagar	pah-gahr	to pay
país (m.)	pah-yees	country
panadería (f.)	pah-nah-deh-ree-yah	bakery
pantalones (m. pl.)	pahn-tah-loh-nehs	pants
papel (m.)	pah-pehl	paper
para	pah-rah	for
parque (m.)	pahr-keh	park
pasar	pah-sahr	to pass, to spend time
película (f.)	peh-lee-koo-lah	film, movie, roll (film)
pelo (m.)	peh-loh	hair
pequeño	peh-keh-nyoh	small
periódico (m.)	peh-ree-oh-dee-koh	newspaper
piso (m.)	pee-soh	floor (story)
pista (f.)	pees-tah	rink, slope, track
poco	poh-koh	little, few
pollo (m.)	poh-yoh	chicken
poner	poh-nehr	to put
por	pohr	along, by, per, through
por favor	pohr fah-bohr	please
por qué	pohr keh	why
precio (m.)	preh-see-yoh	price
preguntar	preh-goon-tahr	to ask
prestar	prehs-tahr	to borrow, to lend
primavera (f.)	pree-mah-beh-rah	spring
primero	pree-meh-roh	first

Spanish	Pronunciation	English
pronóstico (m.)	proh-nohs-tee-koh	weather forecast
pronto	prohn-toh	soon
próximo	prohk-see-moh	next
puerta (f.)	pwehr-tah	door, gate
qué	keh	what
querer	keh-rehr	to want
quién	kee-yehn	who, whom
quince	keen-seh	fifteen
recibir	rreh-see-beer	to receive
recibo (m.)	rreh-see-boh	receipt
reclamo de equipage (m.)	rreh-klah-moh deh eh-kee-pah-heh	bagage claim area
reloj (m.)	rreh-loh	clock, watch
revista (f.)	rreh-bees-tah	magazine
rojo	rroh-hoh	red
ropa (f.)	rroh-pah	clothing
rubio	rroo-bee-yoh	blond
sábado	sah-bah-doh	Saturday
sacar	sah-kahr	to take out
sal (f.)	sahl	salt
salida (f.)	sah-lee-dah	departure, exit, gate
salir	sah-leer	to go out, to leave, to deboard, to exit
salsa (f.)	sahl-sah	sauce
saludar	sah-loo-dahr	greet
sastre (m.)	sahs-treh	suit, tailor
seis	seh-yees	six

Spanish	Pronunciation	English
sello (m.)	seh-yoh	stamp
semana (f.)	seh-mah-nah	week
septiembre	sehp-tee-yehm-breh	September
ser	sehr	to be
sesenta	seh-sehn-tah	sixty
setenta	seh-tehn-tah	seventy
siempre	see-yehm-preh	always
siete	see-yeh-teh	seven
silla (f.)	see-yah	chair
sin	seen	without
sin duda	seen doo-dah	without a doubt
sitio (m.)	see-tee-yoh	sight
sobre	soh-breh	on, upon
subir	soo-beer	to climb, to go up
sucursal (f.)	soo-koor-sahl	branch
sur (m.)	soor	South
tabaquería (f.)	tah-bah-keh-ree-yah	tobacco store
también	tahm-bee-yehn	also, too
tan	tahn	as, so
tarde	tahr-deh	late
tarde (f.)	tahr-deh	afternoon
tarifa	tah-ree-fah	rate
tarjeta (f.)	tahr-heh-tah	card
tasa (f.)	tah-sah	rate
temprano	tehm-prah-noh	early
tener	teh-nehr	to have
tener cuidado	teh-nehr kwee-dah-doh	to be careful

Spanish	Pronunciation	English
tener dolor de	teh-nehr doh-lohr deh	to have an ache in
tener éxito	teh-nehr ehk-see-toh	to succeed
tener ganas de	teh-nehr gah-nahs deh	to feel like
tener lugar	teh-nehr loo-gahr	to take place
tener prisa	teh-nehr pree-sah	to be in a hurry
tener que + infinitive	teh-nehr keh	to have to + infinitive
tener razón	teh-nehr rrah-sohn	to be right
tener __ años	teh-nehr ah-nyohs	to be __ years old
tiempo (m.)	tee-yehm-poh	time, weather
tienda (f.)	tee-yehn-dah	store
tienda de regalos (f.)	tee-yehn-dah deh rreh-gah-lohs	gift shop
tienda de ultramarinos (f.)	tee-yehn-dah deh ool-trah-mah-ree-nohs	delicatessen
tirar	tee-rahr	to pull, to shoot
todavía	toh-dah-bee-yah	still, yet
todo	toh-doh	all
tomar	toh-mahr	to take
traer	trah-yehr	to bring
trece	treh-seh	thirteen
treinta	treh-yeen-tah	thirty
tren (m.)	trehn	train
tres	trehs	three
último	ool-tee-moh	last
uno	oo-noh	one
usar	oo-sahr	to use, wear

Spanish	Pronunciation	English
valer	bah-lehr	to be worth
veinte	behn-teh	twenty
vender	behn-dehr	to sell
venir	beh-neer	to come
venta (f.)	behn-tah	sale
ventana (f.)	behn-tah-nah	window
ventanilla (f.)	behn-tah-nee-yah	window (ticket)
ver	behr	to see
verano (m.)	beh-rah-noh	summer
verde	behr-deh	green
viaje (m.)	bee-yah-heh	trip
viejo	bee-yeh-hoh	old
viernes	bee-yehr-nehs	Friday
vivir	bee-beer	to live
volver	bohl-behr	to return
vuelo (m.)	bweh-loh	flight
ya	yah	already
zapato (m.)	sah-pah-toh	shoe

English–Spanish Dictionary

English	Spanish	Pronunciation
able (to be able)	poder	poh-dehr
about	de, a eso de	deh, ah eh-soh deh
above	encima de	ehn-see-mah deh
to accompany	acompañar	ah-kohm-pah-nyahr
ad	anuncio (m.)	ah-noon-see-yoh
address	dirección (f.)	dee-rehk-see-yohn
to adjust	arreglar	ah-rreh-glahr
advisable	aconsejable	ah-kohn-seh-hah-bleh
after	después (de)	dehs-pwehs (deh)
afternoon	tarde (f.)	tahr-deh
again	de nuevo	deh nweh-boh
against	contra	kohn-trah
ago	hace	ah-seh
to agree with	estar de acuerdo con	ehs-tahr deh ah-kwehr-doh kohn
air conditioning	aire acondicionado (m.)	ah-ee-reh ah-kohn-dee-see-yoh-nah-doh
airline	aerolínea (f.)	ah-yeh-roh-lee-neh-yah
airport	aeropuerto (m.)	ah-yeh-roh-pwehr-toh

English	Spanish	Pronunciation
all	todo	toh-doh
almost	casi	kah-see
already	ya	yah
also	también	tahm-bee-yehn
always	siempre	see-yehm-preh
American consulate	consulado americano (m.)	kohn-soo-lah-doh ah-meh-ree-kah-noh
American embassy	embajada americana (f.)	ehm-bah-hah-dah ah-meh-ree-kah-nah
among	entre	ehn-treh
apple	manzana (f.)	mahn-sah-nah
April	abril	ah-breel
area code	clave de área (f.)	klah-beh deh ah-reh-yah
arm	brazo (m.)	brah-soh
around	alrededor (de)	ahl-reh-deh-dohr (deh)
to arrive	llegar	yeh-gahr
ashtray	cenicero (m.)	seh-nee-seh-roh
to ask	preguntar, pedir	preh-goon-tahr, peh-deer
at	a	ah
August	agosto	ah-gohs-toh
automatic teller machine	cajero automático (m.)	kah-heh-roh ow-toh-mah-tee-koh
bad	malo	mah-loh
bakery	panadería (f.)	pah-nah-deh-ree-yah
ball-point pen	bolígrafo (m.)	boh-lee-grah-foh
band-aid	curita (f.)	koo-ree-tah
bank	banco (m.)	bahn-koh
bathing suit	traje de baño (m.)	trah-heh deh bah-nyoh

English	Spanish	Pronunciation
bathroom	cuarto de baño (m.)	kwahr-toh deh bah-nyoh
bathrooms	baño (m.)	bah-nyoh
to be	estar, ser	ehs-tahr, sehr
beach	playa (f.)	plah-yah
beef	carne de vaca (de res) (f.)	kahr-neh deh bah-kah (deh rrehs)
beer	cerveza (f.)	sehr-beh-sah
before	antes (de)	ahn-tehs (deh)
to begin	comenzar	koh-mehn-sahr
behind	detrás (de)	deh-trahs (deh)
bellman	portero (m.)	pohr-teh-roh
below	debajo de	deh-bah-hoh deh
beneath	debajo de	deh-bah-hoh deh
better	mejor	meh-hohr
between	entre	ehn-treh
big	grande	grahn-deh
bill	factura (f.)	fahk-too-rah
black	negro	neh-groh
blanket	manta (f.)	mahn-tah
blouse	blusa (f.)	bloo-sah
blue	azul	ah-sool
to board	abordar	ah-bohr-dahr
book	libro (m.)	lee-broh
bookstore	librería (f.)	lee-breh-ree-yah
booth (phone)	cabina (casilla) telefónica (f.)	kah-bee-nah (kah-see-yah) teh-leh-foh-nee-kah
to borrow	prestar	prehs-tahr
bottle	botella (f.)	boh-teh-yah

English	Spanish	Pronunciation
box	caja (f.)	kah-hah
branch (office)	sucursal (f.)	soo-koor-sahl
brand name	marca (f.)	mahr-kah
bread	pan (m.)	pahn
to bring	traer	trah-yehr
brother	hermano (m.)	ehr-mah-noh
brown	pardo, marrón	pahr-doh, mah-rrohn
bullfight	corrida de toros (f.)	koh-rree-dah deh toh-rohs
bus	autobús (m.)	ow-toh-boos
butcher shop	carnicería (f.)	kahr-nee-seh-ree-yah
butter	mantequilla (f.)	mahn-teh-kee-yah
button	botón (m.)	boh-tohn
to buy	comprar	kohm-prahr
by	por	pohr
calculator (solar)	calculadora solar (f.)	kahl-koo-lah-doh-rah soh-lahr
to call	telefonear, llamar por teléfono	teh-leh-foh-neh-yahr, yah-mahr pohr teh-leh-foh-noh
camera	cámara (f.)	kah-mah-rah
can	lata (f.)	lah-tah
candy	dulces (m./pl.)	dool-sehs
candy store	confitería (f.)	kohn-fee-teh-ree-yah
car	coche (m.), automóvil (m.), carro (m.)	koh-cheh, ow-toh-moh-beel, kah-rroh
cash	dinero (m.)	dee-neh-roh
to cash a check	cobrar un cheque	koh-brahr oon cheh-keh

English	Spanish	Pronunciation
cashier	cajero (m.)	kah-heh-roh
chair	silla (f.)	see-yah
to change	cambiar	kahm-bee-yahr
change (coins)	moneda (f.)	moh-neh-dah
check	cheque (m.)	cheh-keh
checkbook	chequera (f.)	cheh-keh-rah
cheese	queso (m.)	keh-soh
chicken	pollo (m.)	poh-yoh
church	iglesia (f.)	ee-gleh-see-yah
clock	reloj (m.)	rreh-loh
coffee	café (m.)	kah-feh
cold, to be cold (person)	tener frío	teh-nehr free-yoh
cold, to be cold (weather)	hacer frío	ah-sehr free-yoh
to come	venir	beh-neer
computer	computadora (f.)	kohm-poo-tah-doh-rah
cookie	galleta (f.)	gah-yeh-tah
cordless (portable) phone	teléfono inalámbrico (m.)	teh-leh-foh-noh een-ah-lahm-bree-koh
to cost	costar	kohs-tahr
country	campo (m.), país (m.)	kahm-poh, pah-yees
cup	taza (f.), copa (f.)	tah-sah, koh-pah
customs	aduana (f.)	ah-doo-wah-nah
dark	oscuro	oh-skoo-roh
daughter	hija (f.)	ee-hah

English	Spanish	Pronunciation
day	día (m.)	dee-yah
decaffeinated	descafeinado	dehs-kah-feh-ee-nah-doh
December	diciembre	dee-see-yehm-breh
to decide	decidir	deh-see-deer
to declare	declarar	deh-klah-rahr
delicatessen	tienda de ultra-marinos (f.)	tee-yehn-dah deh ool-trah-mah-ree-nohs
to deliver	entregar	ehn-treh-gahr
deodorant	desodorante (m.)	deh-soh-doh-rahn-teh
department store	almacén (m.)	ahl-mah-sehn
departure	salida (f.)	sah-lee-dah
to deposit	depositar, ingresar	deh-poh-see-tahr, een-greh-sahr
to describe	describir	dehs-kree-beer
to desire	desear	deh-seh-yahr
dessert	postre (m.)	pohs-treh
to dial	marcar	mahr-kahr
difficult	difícil	dee-fee-seel
dirty	sucio (m.)	soo-see-yoh
disagreeable	antipático, desagradable	ahn-tee-pah-tee-koh, deh-sah-grah-dah-bleh
discount	descuento (m.), rabaja (f.)	dehs-kwehn-toh, rrah-bah-hah
to do	hacer	ah-sehr
doctor	doctor (m.), médico (m.)	dohk-tohr, meh-dee-koh
door	puerta (f.)	pwehr-tah
downtown	centro (m.)	sehn-troh

English	Spanish	Pronunciation
dozen	docena (f.)	doh-seh-nah
dress	vestido (m.)	behs-tee-doh
to drink	beber	beh-behr
during	durante	doo-rahn-teh
e-mail	correo electrónico (m.)	koh-rreh-yoh eh-lehk-troh-nee-koh
early	temprano	tehm-prah-noh
to earn	ganar	gah-nahr
East	este (m.)	ehs-teh
easy	fácil	fah-seel
to eat	comer	koh-mehr
egg	huevo (m.)	weh-boh
eight	ocho	oh-choh
eighteen	diez y ocho	dee-yehs ee oh-choh
eighty	ochenta	oh-chen-tah
electricity	electricidad (f.)	eh-lehk-tree-see-dahd
elevator	ascensor (m.)	ah-sehn-sohr
eleven	once	ohn-seh
employee	empleado (m.)	ehm-pleh-yah-doh
to end	terminar, concluir	tehr-mee-nahr, kohn-kloo-eer
to enjoy	gozar	goh-sahr
enough	bastante, suficiente	bahs-tahn-teh, soo-fee-see-yehn-teh
entrance	entrada (f.)	ehn-trah-dah
evening	noche (f.)	noh-cheh
exchange rate	tasa (f.) [tipo (m.)] de cambio	tah-sah [tee-poh] deh kahm-bee-yoh

English	Spanish	Pronunciation
exit	salida (f.)	sah-lee-dah
to explain	explicar	ehs-plee-kahr
facing	frente a	frehn-teh ah
far (from)	lejos (de)	leh-hohs (deh)
father	padre (m.)	pah-dreh
February	febrero	feh-breh-roh
fifteen	quince	keen-seh
fifty	cincuenta	seen-kwehn-tah
to find	hallar, encontrar	ah-yahr, ehn-kohn-trahr
first	primero	pree-meh-roh
fish	pescado (m.)	pehs-kah-doh
fish store	pescadería (f.)	pehs-kah-deh-ree-yah
fitness center	gimnasio (m.)	heem-nah-see-yoh
five	cinco (m.)	seen-koh
to fix	arreglar	ah-rreh-glahr
flight	vuelo (m.)	bweh-loh
floor (story)	piso (m.)	pee-soh
for	para, por	pah-rah, pohr
forty	cuarenta	kwah-rehn-tah
four	cuatro	kwah-troh
fourteen	catorce	kah-tohr-seh
frequently	frecuentemente	freh-kwehn-teh-mehn-teh
Friday	viernes	bee-yehr-nehs
from	de, desde	deh, dehs-deh
front, in front (of)	delante (de)	deh-lahn-teh (deh)
gasoline	gasolina (f.)	gah-soh-lee-nah

English	Spanish	Pronunciation
gate	salida (f.), puerta (f.)	sah-lee-dah, pwehr-tah
gift shop	tienda de regalos (f.)	tee-yehn-dah deh rreh-gah-lohs
to give	dar	dahr
glass	vaso (m.)	bah-soh
glove	guante (m.)	gwahn-teh
to go	ir	eer
to go out	salir	sah-leer
good	bueno	bweh-noh
good morning	buenos días	bweh-nohs dee-yahs
good-bye	adiós	ah-dee-yohs
government employee	empleado del gobierno (m.)	ehm-pleh-yah-doh dehl goh-bee-yehr-noh
gray	gris	grees
green	verde	behr-deh
grocery store	abacería (f.)	ah-beh-seh-ree-yah
hair	pelo (m.)	peh-loh
haircut	corte de pelo (m.)	kohr-teh deh peh-loh
ham	jamón (m.)	hah-mohn
hamburger	hamburguesa (f.)	ahm-bohr-geh-sah
hand	mano (f.)	mah-noh
hanger	percha (f.)	pehr-chah
happy	alegre	ah-leh-greh
hat	sombrero (m.)	sohm-breh-roh
to have	tener	teh-nehr
to have an ache (in)	tener dolor (de)	teh-nehr doh-lohr (deh)

English	Spanish	Pronunciation
to have fun	divertirse *ie	dee-behr-teer-seh
to have to …	tener que + infinitive, deber + infinitive	teh-nehr keh, deh-behr
head	cabeza (f.)	kah-beh-sah
to hear	oír	oh-yeer
heart	corazón (m.)	koh-rah-sohn
hello	hola	oh-lah
to help	ayudar	ah-yoo-dahr
here	aquí	ah-kee
holiday	fiesta (f.)	fee-yehs-tah
to hope	esperar	ehs-peh-rahr
hot, to be hot (person)	tener calor	teh-nehr kah-lohr
hot, to be hot (weather)	hacer calor	ah-sehr kah-lohr
hour	hora (f.)	oh-rah
house	casa (f.)	kah-sah
how	cómo	koh-moh
how much, many	cuánto	kwahn-toh
hundred	ciento	see-yehn-toh
hungry (to be hungry)	tener hambre	teh-nehr ahm-breh
hurry (to be in a hurry)	tener prisa	teh-nehr pree-sah
ice cream	helado (m.)	eh-lah-doh
ice cubes	cubitos de hielo (m./pl.)	koo-bee-tohs deh ee-yeh-loh

English	Spanish	Pronunciation
immediately	inmediatamente, en seguida	een-meh-dee-yah-tah-mehn-teh, ehn seh-gee-dah
in	en	ehn
instead of	en lugar de, en vez de	ehn loo-gahr deh, ehn behs deh
jacket	chaqueta (f.), saco (m.)	chah-keh-tah, sah-koh
January	enero	eh-neh-roh
jar	pomo (m.)	poh-moh
jelly	mermelada (f.)	mehr-meh-lah-dah
jewelry store	joyería (f.)	hoh-yeh-ree-yah
to jog	trotar	troh-tahr
juice	jugo (m.)	hoo-goh
July	julio	hoo-lee-yoh
June	junio	hoo-nee-yoh
to keep	guardar	gwahr-dahr
ketchup	salsa de tomate (f.)	sahl-sah deh toh-mah-teh
key	llave (f.), tecla (f.)	yah-beh, teh-klah
kitchen	cocina (f.)	koh-see-nah
knife	cuchillo (m.)	koo-chee-yoh
lamb	carne de cordero (f.)	kahr-neh deh kohr-deh-roh
lamp	lámpara (f.)	lahm-pah-rah
to land	aterrizar	ah-teh-rree-sahr
to last	durar	doo-rahr
last	pasado, último	pah-sah-doh, ool-tee-moh
late	tarde	tahr-deh

English	Spanish	Pronunciation
late in arriving	en retraso	ehn rreh-trah-soh
laundry	lavandería (f.)	lah-bahn-deh-ree-yah
to learn	aprender	ah-prehn-dehr
leather	cuero (m.)	kweh-roh
leather goods store	marroquinería (f.)	mah-rroh-kee-neh-ree-yah
to leave	dejar, quitar, salir	deh-hahr, kee-tahr, sah-leer
lemon	limón (m.)	lee-mohn
to lend	prestar	prehs-tahr
lens	lente (m.)	lehn-teh
less	menos	meh-nohs
letter	carta (f.)	kahr-tah
light	claro	klah-roh
lighter	encendedor (m.)	ehn-sehn-deh-dohr
to like	gustar	goos-tahr
liquor store	tienda de licores (f.)	tee-yehn-dah deh lee-koh-rehs
to listen to	escuchar	ehs-koo-chahr
little	poco	poh-koh
to live	vivir	bee-beer
long	largo	lahr-goh
to look at	mirar	mee-rahr
to look for	buscar	boos-kahr
to lose	perder	pehr-dehr
lucky (to be lucky)	tener suerte	teh-nehr swehr-teh
machine	máquina (f.)	mah-kee-nah
magazine	revista (f.)	rreh-bees-tah

English	Spanish	Pronunciation
maid	criada (f.)	kree-yah-dah
maid service	gobernanta (f.)	goh-behr-nahn-tah
mailbox	buzón (m.)	boo-sohn
to make	hacer	ah-sehr
makeup	maquillaje (m.)	mah-kee-yah-heh
mall	centro comercial (m.)	sehn-troh koh-mehr-see-yahl
management	gestión (f.)	hehs-tee-yohn
manager	gerente (m.)	heh-rehn-teh
March	marzo	mahr-soh
match	fósforo (m.)	fohs-foh-roh
May	mayo	mah-yoh
mayonnaise	mayonesa (f.)	mah-yoh-neh-sah
to mean	significar	seeg-nee-fee-kahr
menu	carta (f.), menú (m.)	kahr-tah, meh-noo
message	mensaje (m.)	mehn-sah-heh
milk	leche (f.)	leh-cheh
mineral water	agua mineral (m.)	ah-gwah mee-neh-rahl
minute	minuto (m.)	mee-noo-toh
mirror	espejo (m.)	ehs-peh-hoh
Monday	lunes	loo-nehs
money	dinero (m.)	dee-neh-roh
money exchange	cambio de dinero (m.)	kahm-bee-yoh deh dee-neh-roh
month	mes (m.)	mehs
monument	monumento (m.)	moh-noo-mehn-toh
more	más	mahs

English	Spanish	Pronunciation
morning	mañana (f.)	mah-nyah-nah
mother	madre (f.)	mah-dreh
mouthwash	elixir bucal (m.)	eh-leek-seer boo-kahl
movie	película (f.)	peh-lee-koo-lah
movies	cine (m.)	see-neh
museum	museo (m.)	moo-seh-yoh
mushroom	champiñon (m.)	chahm-pee-nyohn
mustard	mostaza (f.)	mohs-tah-sah
napkin	servilleta (f.)	sehr-bee-yeh-tah
near	cerca (de)	sehr-kah (deh)
necessary	necesario	neh-seh-sah-ree-yoh
to need	necesitar	neh-seh-see-tahr
new	nuevo	nweh-boh
news	noticias (f./pl.)	noh-tee-see-yahs
newspaper	periódico (m.)	peh-ree-yoh-dee-koh
newstand	quiosco de periódicos (m.)	kee-yohs-koh deh peh-ree-yoh-dee-kohs
next	próximo	prohk-see-moh
next to	al lado de	ahl lah-doh deh
nice	simpático, amable	seem-pah-tee-koh, ah-mah-bleh
nine	nueve	nweh-beh
nineteen	diez y nueve	dee-yehs ee noo-weh-beh
ninety	noventa	noh-behn-tah
nobody	nadie	nah-dee-yeh
North	norte (m.)	nohr-teh
November	noviembre	noh-bee-yehm-breh
now	ahora	ah-oh-rah
number	número (m.)	noo-meh-roh

English	Spanish	Pronunciation
October	octubre	ohk-too-breh
of	de	deh
of course	por supuesto, claro	pohr soo-pwehs-toh, klah-roh
office	oficina (f.)	oh-fee-see-nah
often	a menudo	ah meh-noo-doh
okay	de acuerdo	deh ah-kwehr-doh
old	viejo	bee-yeh-hoh
on	sobre	soh-breh
one	uno	oo-noh
onion	cebolla (f.)	seh-boh-yah
to open	abrir	ah-breer
opposite	frente a	frehn-teh ah
to order	mandar	mahn-dahr
out of order	fuera de servicio	fweh-rah deh sehr-bee-see-yoh
package	paquete (m.)	pah-keh-teh
pants	pantalones (m. pl.)	pahn-tah-loh-nehs
paper	papel (m.)	pah-pehl
parents	padres (m./pl.)	pah-drehs
park	parque (m.)	pahr-keh
to participate	participar	pahr-tee-see-pahr
passport	pasaporte (m.)	pah-sah-pohr-teh
to pay	pagar	pah-gahr
pencil	lápiz (m.)	lah-pees
pepper	pimienta (f.)	pee-mee-yehn-tah
to phone	telefonear	teh-leh-foh-neh-yahr
phone (public)	teléfono público (m.)	teh-leh-foh-noh poo-blee-koh

English	Spanish	Pronunciation
phone card	tarjeta telefónica (f.)	tahr-heh-tah teh-leh-foh-nee-kah
piece	pedazo (m.)	peh-dah-soh
pill	pastilla (f.)	pahs-tee-yah
pillow	almohada (f.)	ahl-moh-ah-dah
pink	rosado	rroh-sah-doh
place	lugar (m.)	loo-gahr
plane	avión (m.)	ah-bee-yohn
plate	plato (m.)	plah-toh
to play games, sports	jugar	hoo-gahr
please	por favor	pohr fah-bohr
pocketbook	bolsa (f.)	bohl-sah
police officer	agente de policia (m.)	ah-hen-teh deh poh-lee-see-yah
police station	comisaria de policia (f.)	koh-mee-sah-ree-yah deh poh-lee-see-yah
pool	piscina (f.)	pee-see-nah
poor	pobre (f.)	poh-breh
porter	portero (m.)	pohr-teh-roh
postcard	tarjeta postal (f.)	tahr-heh-tah pohs-tahl
postage	franqueo (m.)	frahn-keh-yoh
postal code	código postal (m.)	koh-dee-goh pohs-tahl
potato	papa (f.), patata (f.)	pah-pah, pah-tah-tah
pound	quinientos gramos, libra (f.)	kee-nee-yeh-tohs grah-mohs, lee-brah

English	Spanish	Pronunciation
pretty	bonito	boh-nee-toh
price	precio (m.)	preh-see-yoh
problem	problema (m.)	proh-bleh-mah
to purchase	comprar	kohm-prahr
purple	morado	moh-rah-doh
to put	poner, colocar	poh-nehr, koh-loh-kahr
quickly	rápidamente	rrah-pee-dah-mehn-teh
to read	leer	leh-ehr
receipt	recibo (m.)	rreh-see-boh
to receive	recibir	rreh-see-beer
red	rojo	rroh-hoh
relatives	parientes (m./pl.)	pah-ree-yehn-tehs
to remember	recordar	rreh-kohr-dah
to repair	reparar	rreh-pah-rahr
restaurant	restaurante (m.)	rrehs-tow-rahn-teh
to return	regresar	rreh-greh-sahr
room	cuarto (m.), habitación (f.)	kwahr-toh, ah-bee-tah-see-yohn
safe	caja fuerte (f.)	kah-hah fwehr-teh
sale	venta (f.)	behn-tah
salesperson	vendedor (m.)	behn-deh-dohr
salt	sal (f.)	sahl
salt shaker	salero (m.)	sah-leh-roh
sample	muestra (f.)	mwehs-trah
sandal	sandalia (f.)	sahn-dah-lee-yah
Saturday	sábado	sah-bah-doh
sauce	salsa (f.)	sahl-sah
saucer	platillo (m.)	plah-tee-yoh

English	Spanish	Pronunciation
to say	decir	deh-seer
scissors	tijeras (f./pl.)	tee-heh-rahs
seafood	mariscos (m./pl.)	mah-rees-kohs
seat	asiento (m.)	ah-see-yehn-toh
seat belt	cinturón de seguridad (m.)	seen-too-rohn deh seh-goo-ree-dahd
to see	ver	behr
to sell	vender	behn-dehr
to send	mandar, enviar	mahn-dahr, ehn-bee-yahr
September	septiembre	sehp-tee-yehm-breh
seven	siete	see-yeh-teh
seventeen	diez y siete	dee-yehs ee see-yeh-teh
seventy	setenta	seh-tehn-tah
shampoo anti-dandruff	champú (m.) anti-caspa	chahm-poo ahn-tee kahs-pah
shirt	camisa (f.)	kah-mee-sah
shoe	zapato (m.)	sah-pah-toh
short	bajo, corto	bah-hoh, kohr-toh
to show	enseñar, mostrar	ehn-sehn-nyahr, mohs-trahr
show	espectáculo (m.)	ehs-pehk-tah-koo-loh
sick	enfermo	ehn-fehr-moh
since	desde	dehs-deh
sister	hermana (f.)	ehr-mah-nah
six	seis	seh-yees
sixteen	diez y seis	dee-yehs ee seh-yees
sixty	sesenta	seh-sehn-tah
skirt	falda (f.)	fahl-dah

English	Spanish	Pronunciation
slice	trozo (m.)	troh-soh
slowly	lentamente	lehn-tah-mehn-teh
small	pequeño	peh-keh-nyoh
to smoke	fumar	foo-mahr
sneakers	tenis (m. pl.)	teh-nees
so	tan	tahn
sock	calcetín (m.)	kahl-seh-teen
soda	gaseosa (f.), soda (f.)	gah-seh-yoh-sah, soh-dah
son	hijo (m.)	ee-hoh
soon	pronto	prohn-toh
sour	cortado	kohr-tah-doh
South	sur (m.)	soor
South America	Sudamérica (f.), América del Sur (f.)	sood-ah-meh-ree-kah, ah-meh-ree-kah dehl soor
Spain	España	ehs-pah-nyah
to speak	hablar	hah-blahr
to spend money	gastar	gahs-tahr
to spend time	pasar	pah-sahr
spicy	picante	pee-kahn-teh
spinach	espinaca (f.)	ehs-pee-nah-kah
spot	mancha (f.)	mahn-chah
spring	primavera (f.)	pree-mah-beh-rah
stadium	estadio (m.)	ehs-tah-dee-yoh
stamp	sello (m.)	seh-yoh
still	todavía	toh-dah-bee-yah
stockings	medias (f. pl.)	meh-dee-yahs
stop-over	escala (f.)	ehs-kah-lah

English	Spanish	Pronunciation
store	tienda (f.)	tee-yehn-dah
subway	metro (m.)	meh-troh
sugar	azúcar (m.)	ah-soo-kahr
suitcase	maleta (f.)	mah-leh-tah
summer	verano (m.)	beh-rah-noh
Sunday	domingo	doh-meen-goh
sunglasses	gafas de sol (f./pl.)	gah-fahs deh sohl
suntan lotion	loción de sol (f.), loción para broncearse (f.)	loh-see-yohn deh sohl, loh-see-yohn pah-rah brohn-seh-yahr-seh
supermarket	supermercado (m.)	soo-pehr-mehr-kah-doh
sweater	suéter (m.)	sweh-tehr
sweet	dulce	dool-seh
swimming pool	piscina (f.)	pee-see-nah
T-shirt	camiseta (f.), playera (f.)	kah-mee-seh-tah, plah-yeh-rah
table	mesa (f.)	meh-sah
to take	tomar	toh-mahr
to take place	tener lugar	teh-nehr loo-gahr
to talk	hablar	hah-blahr
tall	alto	ahl-toh
tax	impuesto (m.)	eem-pwehs-toh
taxi	taxi (m.)	tahk-see
tea	té (m.)	teh
teaspoon	cucharita (f.)	koo-chah-ree-tah
telephone	teléfono (m.)	teh-leh-foh-noh
to telephone	telefonear	teh-leh-foh-neh-yahr

English	Spanish	Pronunciation
telephone book	guía telefónica (f.)	gee-yah teh-leh-foh-nee-kah
telephone number	número de teléfono (m.)	noo-meh-roh deh teh-leh-foh-noh
television (color)	televisión en color (f.)	teh-leh-bee-see-yohn ehn koh-lohr
to tell	decir	deh-seer
ten	diez	dee-yehs
thank you	muchas gracias	moo-chahs grah-see-yahs
theater	teatro (m.)	teh-yah-troh
then	pues	pwehs
there	allá	ah-yah
thirteen	trece	treh-seh
thirty	treinta	treh-een-tah
thousand	mil	meel
three	tres	trehs
throat	garganta (f.)	gar-gahn-tah
through	por	pohr
Thursday	jueves	hoo-weh-behs
ticket	boleto (m.)	boh-leh-toh
time	tiempo (m.), hora (f.)	tee-yehm-poh, oh-rah
time (at what time?)	a qué hora	ah keh oh-rah
time (on time)	a tiempo	ah tee-yem-poh
tip	propina (f.)	proh-pee-nah
tissue	pañuelo de papel (m.)	pah-nyoo-weh-loh deh pah-pehl
to	a	ah

English	Spanish	Pronunciation
tobacco store	tabaquería (f.)	tah-bah-keh-ree-yah
today	hoy	oy
tomato	tomate (m.)	toh-mah-teh
tomorrow	mañana	mah-nyah-nah
too	también	tahm-bee-yehn
too much	demasiado	deh-mah-see-yah-doh
tooth	diente (m.)	dee-yehn-teh
toothbrush	cepillo de los dientes (m.)	seh-pee-yoh deh lohs dee-yehn-tehs
toothpaste	pasta dentifrica (f.)	pahs-tah dehn-tee-free-kah
towel	toalla (f.)	toh-wah-yah
train	tren (m.)	trehn
to travel	viajar	bee-yah-hahr
traveler's check	cheque de viajero (m.)	cheh-keh deh bee-yah-heh-roh
trip	viaje (m.)	bee-yah-heh
Tuesday	martes	mahr-tehs
turkey	pavo (m.)	pah-boh
twelve	doce	doh-seh
twenty	veinte	behn-teh
two	dos	dohs
umbrella	paraguas (m.)	pah-rah-gwahs
under	debajo de	deh-bah-hoh deh
to understand	comprender, entender	kohm-prehn-dehr, ehn-tehn-dehr
United States	Estados Unidos (m./pl.)	ehs-tah-dohs oo-nee-dohs
until	hasta	ahs-tah
to use	usar	oo-sahr

English	Spanish	Pronunciation
vegetable	legumbre (f.)	leh-goom-breh
very	muy	mwee
to visit	visitar	bee-see-tahr
to wait for	esperar	ehs-peh-rahr
wallet	cartera (f.)	kahr-teh-rah
to want	querer	keh-rehr
weather	tiempo (m.)	tee-yehm-poh
weather forecast	pronóstico (m.)	proh-nohs-tee-koh
Wednesday	miércoles	mee-yehr-koh-lehs
week	semana (f.)	seh-mah-nah
welcome (you're welcome)	bienvenido de nada	byehn-beh-nee-doh deh nah-dah
well	bien	byehn
West	oeste (m.)	oh-wehs-teh
what	qué	keh
when	cuándo	kwahn-doh
where	dónde	dohn-deh
which	cuál	kwahl
while	rato (m.)	rrah-toh
white	blanco	blahn-koh
who(m)	quién	kee-yehn
why	por qué	pohr keh
winter	invierno (m.)	een-bee-yehr-noh
without	sin	seen
to work	funcionar, trabajar	foonk-see-yoh-nahr, trah-bah-hahr
to write	escribir	ehs-kree-beer

English	Spanish	Pronunciation
yellow	amarillo	ah-mah-ree-yoh
yesterday	ayer	ah-yehr
young	joven	hoh-behn

Index